THE REGIONAL ARTS OF THE EARLY SOUTH

THE REGIONAL ARTS
OF THE EARLY SOUTH

A Sampling from the Collection of the Museum of
Early Southern Decorative Arts

JOHN BIVINS AND FORSYTH ALEXANDER

Published by the Museum of Early Southern Decorative Arts

Winston-Salem, North Carolina

Distributed by The University of North Carolina Press

Chapel Hill and London

Design: Kachergis Book Design, Pittsboro, N.C.
Cover design: John Bivins
Photography: the MESDA staff
Typesetting: Graphic Composition, Inc., Athens, Georgia
Printed and bound in Japan

LIBRARY OF CONGRESS CATALOGING-IN-PUBLICATION DATA
Museum of Early Southern Decorative Arts.
    The regional arts of the early South : a sampling from the
  collection of the Museum of Early Southern Decorative Arts / John
  Bivins and Forsyth Alexander.
      p.   cm.
   ISBN 0-945578-02-4 : $24.95
    1. Decorative arts, Early American—Southern States—Catalogs.
  2. Regionalism in art—Catalogs.   3. Decorative arts—North
  Carolina—Winston Salem—Catalogs.   4. Museum of Early Southern
  Decorative Arts—Catalogs.   I. Bivins, John, 1940– .
  II. Alexander, Forsyth, 1960– .   III. Title.
  NK811.M87   1991
   745′.0975′07475667—dc20   91-60524

The preparation of this work has been made possible in part through research
grants from the Research Tools and Reference Works Program of the National
Endowment for the Humanities, an independent Federal agency. The research
collation, analysis, and graphic presentation represent the combined efforts of
the professional staff of the Museum of Early Southern Decorative Arts:

Forsyth Alexander, *Director of Publications*
Whaley Batson, *Paintings Consultant*
Nancy Bean, *Office Manager*
John Bivins, *Adjunct Curator*
Ruth Brooks, *Associate in Education*
Sally Gant, *Director of Education and Special Events*
Paula Hooper, *Coordinator of Membership Services*
Frank L. Horton, *Director Emeritus*
Madelyn Moeller, *Director*
Bradford L. Rauschenberg, *Director of Research*
Martha Rowe, *Research Associate*
Wesley Stewart, *Photographer*
Margaret Vincent, *Collections Manager*
And the MESDA interpretive staff.

CONTENTS

MESDA AND ITS SOUTH

THE SOUTHERN REGIONS
~CHESAPEAKE
~LOW COUNTRY
~BACK COUNTRY

MESDA MUSEUM OF EARLY SOUTHERN DECORATIVE ARTS

Boundaries of the United States as shown in Mitchell's Travellers Guide ~ 1837

MESDA and Its South

The Museum of Early Southern Decorative Arts, a division of Old Salem, Inc., is a young institution. Nevertheless, thanks to the diversity of its programs, it has become recognized as the center for the study of the early arts of the South.

MESDA is the brainchild of Frank L. Horton, who, with his mother, Theo L. Taliaferro, provided the core of the museum's exhibition material from their own advanced collection of southern arts of all sorts, including architectural interiors, certainly the largest such privately held collection in existence. With an initial endowment also provided by Horton and his mother, the museum grew inside the shell of what had been a grocery store located in the southern environs of the present Old Salem historic district, which at the time was undergoing a long process of restoration. MESDA opened its doors in January 1965.

Frank Horton's goals for the museum were ambitious. Aside from the constant strengthening of the institution's collection, he envisioned an all-encompassing research program that would not only reveal the names of anonymous southern artisans, but also provide a sound interpretation of the museum's collections. Natural complements to such a program, as Horton saw it, were publications.

The care, interpretation, and development of the new museum's collection were its first priorities. Research was its second, but equal in importance. A two-part research program was planned. One part was designed to locate and record examples of southern material culture—decorative arts made in the South—from Maryland to Georgia and west to Kentucky. The second part provided for primary research in the public and private records of every county of the early South: Maryland, Virginia, the Carolinas, Georgia, Tennessee, and Kentucky. Both of these programs were initiated in the early 1970s and funded for a decade by the National Endowment for the Humanities.

Much of the planned field research was complete by 1985. Over 15,000 objects had been recorded and photographed by then, and this work still continues. The documentary research, owing to the enormous quantity of records that require examination, will continue for many years. MESDA's file of southern artisans and artists working through 1820 now contains biographical information on over 60,000 persons working in 125 different trades. A computerized database provides an index of all the information available in the main file for each artisan. Both the object files and the research data are open to the public and constantly provide new material for publications, including MESDA's *Journal of Early Southern Decorative Arts* and the books of the Frank L. Horton Series.

At the outset, MESDA's South required geographic and cultural definition. The French settlements of the Mississippi Valley, although of considerable importance in the production of early arts, were deemed too far afield. The Deep South, Alabama and Mississippi, was excluded on other grounds: except for a few coastal and river towns, this area was settled relatively late and principally by planters from the upper South. MESDA's chief concern was with objects—furniture, metalwares and textiles of all sorts, ceramics, and fine art—that exhibited unique southern styles. In general, such objects were made before the 1820s. After about 1820, owing to vastly improved transportation systems, regional designs gave way increasingly to national trends, at least in the coastal South.

MESDA exists for its public's benefit. But it also exists for and because of people long gone, the artisans and their patrons, and the cultures that defined them and gave rise to what we now think of as southern decorative art. For the most part, these objects were seen as *applied* art by those who made and owned them. They were intended, among other things, to be useful. They were the products of a tightly interwoven tapestry of tradition that contained threads of an international sense of design flow, utility, and technology.

How these factors came together to create regional design, whether academic or vernacular, whether a great classical James River brick manor in the Palladian style or a humble earthenware storage jar from a Tennessee cove, should be understood within the context of people: where they came from, what they needed, what

they valued. The ebb and flow of productivity, the presence of design sources or even the distance from them, is written in the history of settlement patterns and regional economies, in the presence or lack of useful transportation, and in the cultural roots of the settlers. No matter how far back in time we may pursue the arts of any region of the South, we find that we cannot ignore these roots. It is not enough to know that an artisan was English. Was he from London, or one of the lesser shires, or even the rural West Country? For that matter, was he even English? Mightn't he have been Irish, Welsh, or Scottish? If we can hope for sound answers to such questions, then we have far greater ability to understand the development of style in the South—or any other region of the world, for that matter. The business of MESDA, then, is not only object studies, but social history.

When MESDA opened its doors to the public in 1965, not a single object in the collection could be confidently attributed to a specific maker. Since then, documentary research has assisted us in attributing scores of objects, and field research has unearthed a significant number of signed works in every medium. The blending of these research programs, virtually unparalleled elsewhere, also has enormously strengthened our ability to perceive southern-made objects as documents, no less so in many instances than recorded history. The dissemination of the unique taste and style of a seventeenth-century Quaker settlement in Maryland, for example, is evident in the sure hand of an unknown turner who made both the legs of a bold gateleg table (1) and the crisp gallery balusters of Old Third Haven Meeting in Easton (2), constructed in the 1680s. Three-quarters of a century later, and further down the Chesapeake, an emigrant

1

3

2

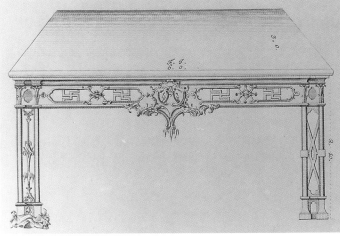

4

Englishman named William Buckland was gaining stature as an architect. He was engaged by John Tayloe of Mount Airy to design the interiors of his elegant stone manor. Consulting his own volume of Thomas Chippendale's *Gentleman and Cabinet Maker's Director*, Buckland followed the tradition of British architects such as William Kent by designing Tayloe's furnishings as well. A magnificent slab table (3) was one result, translated from Chippendale's composition (4) by the table's carver, William Bernard Sears.

The migratory flight of international style in the arts is not well understood, and therefore stylistic terminology often has been oversimplified, particularly in the case of American furniture, where, in the past, descriptions have been placed under the umbrella of English culture. For example, terms such as "Queen Anne" or "Chippendale" have been applied to objects whose stylistic roots lie entirely on the Continent. We find that an art-historical approach does more justice to the complexities of the situation. Indeed, calling an object "late

Baroque" instead of "Queen Anne," or "Rococo" instead of "Chippendale," solves diverse problems. For example, we've never had a Chippendale teapot, but there have been plenty of Rococo examples.

The presence of objects alone often may serve as the only documentation of the origins of design. It is no accident that an eighteenth-century oak chest of drawers (5) recorded by the MESDA staff in Norwich, Norfolk, England, has a distinctive hinged cabinet door like a Mecklenburg County, Virginia, piece (6) of 1800–1801. That the Virginia example is one of a number of such chests suggests that a cabinetmaker trained in the shire of Norfolk had sought a new life in America, bringing with him a tradition that remained foreign to other parts of eastern America. The rapid transmission of far more urban designs is dramatically illustrated by furniture made in southern coastal cabinetmaking centers. Williamsburg, although the capital of Virginia, was a very small town by Philadelphia standards, yet its artisans were capable of London-quality work, as an extensively fretted mahogany tea table (7) amply documents. The "Gothick" taste espoused by Chippendale and his contemporaries is uniquely manifested in a Charleston sideboard table (8) that has no known American parallel.

Even the specialization that marked the urban trades of Britain and the Continent was not without representation in the early South. John Lord, an English carver who emigrated to the Low Country in the 1760s, proudly announced that he had been associated with some of the "best shops in London" and would carry out "gilding and all branches of house and furniture carving, in the Chinese, French, and Gothic tastes." The Corinthian-order modillions (9) of the parlor entablature of Miles Brewton's famed Charleston residence were executed by a carver, perhaps Lord or one of his contemporaries, who also decorated an exquisite Charleston tea table (10).

5

6

7

9

8

10

11

12

Of surviving southern material culture, furniture inevitably represents the largest sampling. Furniture was necessary for even the humblest household, whereas arts such as portraiture were luxuries that fewer people could afford. Nevertheless, MESDA field research has recorded a considerable number of paintings and has brought new attention to such little-known southern artists as John Durand, who in 1769 captured the likeness of Elizabeth Boush (11) of Norfolk. A host of finely worked textiles ranging from samplers to elaborate white-on-white coverlets have been examined, and the existence of exceptionally fragile documents such as a magnificent eighteenth-century silk-on-silk embroidered valentine (12) from Virginia has been recorded for posterity. Southern metalwares ranging from simple cast-iron firebacks to the earliest objects of silver made by southern artisans have been recorded, among them such monumental pieces as a racing trophy (13) by Burnett & Rigden of Georgetown that commemorates the victory of Colonel Wade Hampton's bay Vingt-Un in the Washington Cup of 1803.

Some of the most remarkable objects are the products not of refined urban skills, but of gifted rural tradesmen. Both whimsy and substantial technical ability elevate a piedmont Virginia salt-glazed stoneware figure jug (14) far above the mundane world of everyday crockery. And even in final repose, the German settler of Backcountry North Carolina who so loved color and "fancy" in the objects he'd lived with could be remembered in the finest imaginable fashion (15) by the community's stonecutter.

The objects recorded in MESDA's research files and exhibited in its collection, then, serve as tangible documents of the cultural diversity of the immense region of America known as the South. In the decade following the Revolution, the five southern states—Kentucky and Tennessee were admitted to the Union during the following decade—constituted a land mass one-and-one-half times greater than that of the eight northern states. The South contained more than half the population of the new Republic, yet it was not a region known for large urban centers. During the colonial period, the South had only two cities—Norfolk and Charleston—that could compare with even the medium-sized cities of the North. The ruralness of the region was overwhelming. In 1733 Royal Governor George Burrington had aptly characterized the vastness of just one of the southern colonies: "Land is not wanting for men in Carolina, but men for land."

13

14

15

Towns did develop, and grew into cities, but the essentially agrarian nature of the South persisted. Even today town-dwelling southerners tend to retain a strong nostalgic tie with the land and "an ineradicable sense of place," as one contemporary writer has put it. We generally associate the development of trades—and therefore the decorative arts—with the presence of centers of commerce, but the early rural South nevertheless managed to attract skilled tradesmen, even from northern cities. This attraction had a solid economic basis, as we learn from a frustrated census-taker, who, in 1820, found it "impossible to get even the proceeds" of various trades, for the tradesmen were "Summer Agricultorists and Winter Mechanicks." The southern farmer-artisan's way to financial success lay not just in extensive patronage, but in a handsome parcel of acreage as well.

By no means culturally monolithic, the South was composed of three distinct regions: the Chesapeake, the Low Country, and the Backcountry. A sharp cultural contrast between these regions was evident by the second quarter of the eighteenth century. A James River planter would have scoffed at a two-story log dwelling considered elegant by a successful Catawba Valley farmer. A Tennessee mountain man, comfortable with his graceful iron-mounted longrifle and tomahawk, would not have been caught dead wearing the expensive silver-mounted small-sword so favored by Charleston gentlemen. The separateness of the three regions is central to MESDA's interpretation and education programs and has dictated the format of this catalog. Yet we can find a degree of design transmission from region to region, and that makes the picture even more interesting.

Join us, then, in a tour of MESDA's South: a cruise on the Chesapeake, a round of visits in the townhouses and plantations of the Carolina Low Country, and an exploration of the endless ridges and verdant rolling hills of the Backcountry. Our true hosts along this route are long gone, but they speak to us through the objects they have left behind.

THE CHESAPEAKE

The Chesapeake

Enticements to settle the southern colonies abounded from the seventeenth century and later. A "Friendly Perswasive" of 1705 was typical of most, extolling the "clear and serene Air" and the "vast quantities of Timber for Shipping, Trade, and Architecture." The most telling description of the Chesapeake, however, was that it was "a Bay in most respects scarcer to be outdone by the Universe." Water indeed dominated everything in the Chesapeake South. It not only provided ready transportation and fine maritime commerce; it also formed and defined the quality of the land, from grassy pocosins and cypress swamps to the rich river-borne loam that made intensive cultivation possible. The combination of climate, soil, and the vast network of waterways together shaped the development of Chesapeake settlement and culture from Maryland to the central coast of North Carolina. North Carolina, of course, geographically had nothing to do with the Chesapeake Bay, but emigrants from the Bay area settled there even during the seventeenth century, carrying with them a tradition in the arts and architecture already familiar in Maryland and Virginia.

"Planters can deliver their Commodities at their own Back doors, as the whole Colony is interflow'd by the most navigable Rivers in the World," was the way one correspondent described the Chesapeake scene just before the middle of the eighteenth century. The efficient waterways, however, ironically proved a detriment to the growth of urban centers in the colonial Chesapeake. The same writer observed of the planters: "Being so well seated at home, they have no Ambition to fill a Metropolis, and associate together. For this reason, the Capitals and other Towns . . . are very slightly peopled . . . and remarkable for little else than the Residence of the Governors."

Tobacco, the staple crop that brought enormous wealth to the colonial Chesapeake, further encouraged this phenomenon. The acquisition of vast acreage and the slaves necessary for the production of the labor-intensive crop provided large plantations with a considerable degree of self-sufficiency on one hand, and at the same time made them a tight extension of the Crown's mercantilist trade policies. Tobacco carried a bounty, for it represented the ideal unit of trade: raw goods sent from the colonies for finishing and resale by the English establishment. Fortunes rose and fell with the quality and quantity of tobacco produced. The planters' dependence on their British factors in the handling of their overseas affairs ensured close cultural ties between the Chesapeake and Britain, in contrast with the relative economic independence of the northern colonies.

The result was the demand for modish designs, whether in movables or architecture. In America, the Chesapeake was at the forefront in eagerly embracing the new translations of the classical style that flourished in England at the end of the seventeenth century. The handsome manors and furnishings of Chesapeake planters reflected the academic styles published by the great Baroque designers of London as fresh interpretations of Palladio's *Four Books of Architecture*.

It long has been assumed that the apparent self-sufficiency of the large Chesapeake estates, coupled with the constant commerce with Britain directly from plantation wharves and King's Landings and the resulting small size of Chesapeake towns, did little to encourage the development of trades. Some contemporary writings even appear to confirm that, such as Robert Beverly's well-known 1705 condemnation of his fellow Virginians: "They have all their Wooden Ware from *England*; their Cabinets, Chairs, Tables, Stools, Chests . . . to the Eternal Reproach of their Laziness." The scholarship of the past thirty years, however, has revealed that this gap in the trades scarcely survived the seventeenth century. Research also indicates that slave artisans capable of making household articles were more important to the urban scene than to the plantation. The small towns of the Chesapeake did indeed contain tradesmen patronized by wealthy planters, and in some areas the countryside was dotted with tradesmen's shops as well.

Coastal North Carolina had little of the wealth of the landed tobacco aristocracy of Maryland and Virginia, its tobacco production being both indifferent and meager. Further, as a consequence of its treacherous inlets to the Atlantic, the colony had even fewer towns.

Criss Cross great hall, New Kent County, Virginia, c. 1680.

Criss Cross Hall exterior, New Kent County, Virginia, c. 1680.

Coastal Carolina was best characterized as an emerging society, yet the well-populated hinterland of the Albemarle Sound region supported a significant number of mechanics, particularly cabinetmakers. These artisans often practiced allied trades, including finish carpentry and the production of ship's tackle and riding chairs. More specialized trades generally were absent in the countryside. One English traveler observed in the 1770s that "hosiers, haberdashers, clothiers, linen-drapers, stationers, &c. are not known here; they are all comprehended in the single name and occupation of merchant, or store-keeper."

Chesapeakers considered themselves first and foremost British citizens and as such entitled to the sacred rights shared by every subject of the Crown. One such right was individual independence. William Byrd II wrote from Westover in 1735: "Our Government . . . is

Pocomoke House exterior, Somerset County, Maryland, 1700–1725.

so happily constituted, that a Governour must first, out wit us, before he can oppress us, And if ever he squeeze money out of us, He must first take care to deserve it." This attitude later was to make fierce patriots of the men who fancied that their rights had been trampled under the foot of the Crown.

British tastes in living indeed were prevalent in the Chesapeake. Although planters like Byrd believed that "expence upon our Habitations is certainly the most laudable instance of Luxury," the prevailing preference in the Chesapeake, as in Britain, was for household goods that were "neat," or elegantly sound, in a "plain," or conservative, style. This attitude is evident in a 1772 letter from Robert Beverly II of Blandfield, who seemed to confirm his grandfather's complaint that Virginians "have all their Wooden Ware" from abroad: "I have been some Time employed in building a House, & as I am

Pocomoke room, Somerset County, Maryland, 1700–1725.

Chowan room, Gates County, North Carolina, 1755.

Chowan House exterior, Gates County, North Carolina, 1755.

desirous of fitting it up in a plain neat Manner, I would willingly consult the present Fashion." Ordering furniture from London, despite scattered documents such as Beverly's order, was not common among Chesapeake planters. Beverly himself owned Virginia-made furniture.

Charles Carroll of Annapolis expressed the same sentiment about style in a letter to his son that was written the same year as Beverly's order. Carroll observed that "a rich side board Elegant & Costly furniture May gratify our Pride and Vanity, they may Excite the Praise & admiration of Spectators." But Carroll admonished his son to "enjoy yr Fortune, keep an Hospitable table, But lay out as little money as Possible in dress Furniture & shew of any Sort, decency is the only Point to be aimed at."

Cherry Grove parlor, Northampton County, Virginia, c. 1759.

Although ostentation may have been looked upon with disfavor in the Chesapeake, an appreciation for current fashion and knowledge certainly was not. It was not unusual for a Chesapeake planter to own a very substantial library or to educate his sons in London. On a per capita basis, Chesapeake artisans owned more published design books such as Chippendale's *Director* than many other areas of eastern America. Williamsburg cabinetmakers offered designs current in London and were quick to shun outmoded forms. For example, the cabriole high chest—"highboy" in popular terminology—disappeared in the lower Chesapeake by 1740, just as it did in London.

The Revolution brought radical changes to the makeup of the Chesapeake. As late as 1785, its chief port, Norfolk, remained "a vast heap of Ruins and Devasta-

Cherry Grove House exterior, Northampton County, Virginia, c. 1759.

Edgecombe room, Edgecombe County, North Carolina, 1760–80.

Edgecombe House exterior, Edgecombe County, North Carolina, 1760–80.

tion," and the city emerged from its ashes to find that its patterns of commerce had forever changed. Tobacco declined as the staple crop of Virginia and Maryland, overtaken in the marketplace by grains. The cultivation of wheat and corn required less slave labor, which was expensive, yet because of its bulk required additional shipping. Grain production therefore encouraged shipbuilding and the maritime trade as well, and in turn provided a new impetus to trades such as cabinetmaking.

The cities that exported grain were not the old tobacco ports, but the fast-growing newer towns on the upper James, Richmond and Petersburg, and the emerging ports of the northern Chesapeake such as Baltimore and Alexandria. Baltimore, a mere village in the mid-eighteenth century, at the end of the colonial period gave the appearance of "entirely a Place calculated for

Edenton parlor, Edenton, North Carolina, c. 1766.

Blair-Pollock House exterior, Edenton, North Carolina, c. 1766.

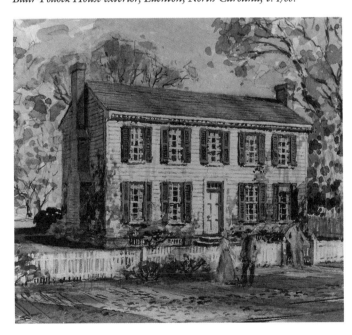

Trade." Norfolk returned to prosperity, owing in no small measure to the burgeoning West Indian trade and overland commerce with North Carolina, but other Chesapeake towns fared less well. A visitor to Williamsburg, which had lost the seat of government to Richmond, reported in 1795 that "not a few private house[s] have tumbled down; others are daily crumbling into ruin."

The North Carolina towns, particularly the ports of Edenton and New Bern, continued to grow modestly after the Revolution, yet their trade continued to be plagued by a lack of staple exports. The forbidding Outer Banks, whose few inlets permitted only shipping of light burden to reach the sounds, continued to discourage transatlantic commerce. After completion of the Dismal Swamp Canal and the Panic of 1819, these small ports fell into a state of somnolence. A reporter

Oxford parlor, Oxford, North Carolina, c. 1815.

Oxford House exterior, Oxford, North Carolina, c. 1815.

wryly remarked in 1857 that Edenton Bay was "all the prettier for not being interrupted by those forests of shipping that mar the appearance of seaport towns."

The arts of the Chesapeake increasingly had shifted to the new urban centers capable of supporting the highly specialized nature of trades such as cabinetmaking. In 1820 Baltimore could boast of over 360 artisans working in that trade, but the entire Albemarle region of North Carolina, reaching from the sound to over 75 miles inland, supported no more than 90 cabinetmakers between 1800 and 1820. The dramatic expansion of the cabinet trade in Philadelphia and New York made itself heavily felt in the increasing imports of northern furniture by the smaller ports of the Chesapeake. No matter how skilled, cabinetmakers in these towns simply could not compete with large urban establishments more attuned to the new technology required by the Neoclassical style.

I

Baluster, Isle of Wight County, Virginia, 1640–60. In the seventeenth century, turners and joiners were required to be exceptionally versatile, able to produce both furniture and architectural elements. This white oak baluster is one of two surviving from St. Luke's Church, constructed in 1632 and still standing. Its interior was not completed until after 1650; the baluster was removed in 1845. Its original location in the church is unknown.

Gift of the Connecticut Historical Society, accession (acc.) 3591. JB

2, 3, 4

Three armchairs. The most formal chairs of the seventeenth century were those with paneled, or wainscot, backs, such as the "great Joyned Chaire" that George Nicholls of Virginia mentioned in his 1677 will. Most of the "great" chairs listed in early records were turned, or post-and-round. A cherry chair of 1680–1700 from southeastern Virginia (2, left) is the earliest such southern example known. The Mannerist form of the turnings, the tall back spindles positioned between two horizontal rounds, and the arms projecting over the front posts are Continental features. The space between the bottom round of the back and the seat suggests the use of a thick squab or cushion. The finials have been shortened. *Acc. 3899.*

Far more in the British tradition, but with arms that project over the posts—a detail common on southern chairs but unknown on northern pieces—a northeastern North Carolina chair of 1690–1700 (3, below left) is made entirely of mulberry except for its base rounds and seat lists. Mulberry is indigenous to the entire east coast, but it appears to have been favored only by southern turners. *Acc. 2024-2.*

One of a number of associated chairs from the area of Mecklenburg County in southeastern Virginia, a maple and oak armchair of 1700–1720 (4, below right) reveals in the form of its back—four rails interspersed with turned spindles—evidence of French styles in the Chesapeake South. Its vasiform post turnings and finials, however, are related to early chairs made in eastern Connecticut. *Acc. 2024-9.* JB

5   Gateleg table, southeastern Virginia, 1675–1700. The inventory of Thomas Walke of Princess Anne County, Virginia, was taken in 1695, listing among other things a "Small Ovall black wallnutt Table." The use of walnut throughout this table, including the gate frames, is common to lower Chesapeake furniture but seldom seen in the North. The butt joints of the table leaves suggest an early date, since later tables have tongue-and-groove joints. The gateleg table represents a seventeenth-century shift toward portability in furniture, in contrast with the more ponderous and "fixed" nature of Renaissance pieces such as trestle tables. *Acc. 950-1.*   *JB*

6   Court cupboard, southeastern Virginia, 1660–80. Of oak and yellow pine with ebonized split spindles and bosses, this court cupboard is one of only two southern examples known. It is the only American cupboard recorded that has an open display shelf over a cabinet; the reverse is usual, and some British examples are open both above and below. Court cupboards were common in early inventories of the more affluent Virginia households and are generally listed with a cupboard cloth. Thomas Walke owned a "plaine Court Cubboard of Virga. Worke with a drawer to it" and an "old Cupboard Cloath wth. Stripes and Shaggs." These cupboards may have been considered "sideboards," even in the seventeenth century; the 1671 inventory of William Moseley of Virginia listed a "side Boarde & Cloathe." William Fitzhugh of the same colony wrote in 1688: "I esteem it as well politic as reputable to furnish myself with a handsom Cupboard of plate." Fitzhugh owned 122 objects of silver at his death, far more than the households of most Chesapeake gentry, which tended to be quite spartan. This example descended from Thomas Vines of York County, Virginia, who died in 1737. *Acc. 2024-6.*   *JB*

7 Clothes press, southeastern Virginia, 1690–1710. In 1671 William Moseley's estate in Norfolk County, Virginia, contained a "greate Dutch Cash" worth 500 pounds of tobacco, a common medium of exchange in the Chesapeake. Both the Germans and the Dutch were fond of large case pieces that served as closets and storage space for folded fabrics, but such presses were rare in seventeenth-century America. Moseley's "Cash" almost certainly represents a corruption of the Dutch *kas*. The dovetail-joined carcass and raised door panels with lip-molded surrounds are the latest features of this walnut and yellow pine press, which indeed may represent either French or Low Countries influence. The asymmetry of its facade suggests the latter. The left side contains shelving, and the right a pegboard for articles to be hung. The feet are not original to the piece and may have been later additions. *Acc. 2024-1.* JB

8 Chest, northeastern North Carolina, 1690–1720. Although this chest has a North Carolina history, it is often difficult to determine whether such an early piece is from Virginia or North Carolina. Francis Simpson of Norfolk County died in 1696, and among his household goods was "One great Old Wainscott Chest 15s." Wainscot was an ancient term derived from the frame-and-panel construction of wagon beds. The walnut, yellow pine, and poplar chest illustrated here actually is of joined construction; i.e., the entire frame is contiguous and joined together with mortise and tenon joints. An unusual detail is the raised panels, which are seldom seen in American furniture made before 1700 but were in use on the Continent before 1650. Also foreign to the tradition of American joined chests is the rail mortised between the front stiles below the drawer, a feature suggesting the beginning of a stylistic transition from joined furniture to dovetailed carcasses fitted with applied bracket feet. A single large dovetail joins each corner of the drawer frame, and the drawer sides are of walnut, a common lower Chesapeake application. The turned feet are not attached to the carcass, and their age is uncertain. *Acc. 2024-5.* JB

9 Sundial, British or American, 1709. Bearing the engraved inscriptions "Vita Umbra" and "Latt 37" along with the date, this sundial, latitude 37 degrees, has a calibration that corresponds precisely with the port of Norfolk. The significance of the initials "IW" is unknown, but the object descended in the Willoughby family; Ensign Willoughby arrived in Norfolk in 1710. The engraving of the chapter ring, although simply ornamented, was the work of a skilled engraver familiar with the finishing of clock faces.

On loan to the museum, acc. 3842.   JB

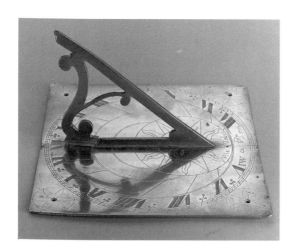

10 Dressing table, northeastern North Carolina or southeastern Virginia, 1710–30. This walnut and yellow pine table is the only known example of a cross-stretcher dressing table made in the South. Its turnings have little of the bold and crisp architectural detail characteristic of Baroque English and northern American tables and high chests, revealing the work of a turner not trained in an urban center. The drawer is rabbeted and nailed at the corners. Typical of the period are the sides of the table frame, which have less height than the front, thereby exposing the drawer supports. A very unusual detail is the cross stretcher, which joins the legs with a rounded boss rather than a square. "Dressing" or "chamber" tables are seldom described in early inventories, very likely because tables of this sort had other uses as well, notably as writing tables. *Acc. 1057.*   JB

11 Stretcher table, northeastern North Carolina, 1720–40. Two aspects of this table suggest an early date: its history of Halifax County in the Roanoke River basin, and its Mannerist turnings. An eighteenth-century date, however, is indicated by the stretchers, which are well under half the thickness of the leg squares. The table is made of sweet gum, a wood that has been observed only in North Carolina furniture dating well before the mid-eighteenth century. *Acc. 2024-25.*   JB

eake

12 Stretcher table, northeastern North Carolina, 1730–40. The simple columnar leg turnings of this walnut table illustrate the conservative but formal recognition of the classical orders typical of early-eighteenth-century lower Chesapeake architecture and furniture; northern turned work, by contrast, is usually Mannerist in form. The flush drawer and heavy stretchers are typical of the first quarter of the century, but the delicate ovolo moldings edging the stretchers and top suggest a slightly later date. Typical of tables from this region, this example is fully finished on the back, with the molding run on the rear edge of the top. *Acc. 2347.* *JB*

13 Infant bed, northeastern North Carolina, 1745–75. Several examples of open-sided beds like this one have been recorded in the lower Chesapeake, although the form is rare in America. Used like cribs, these small beds were drawn to the side of a full-sized bed when in use. Wear on the front rail of this example indicates that it also has been used as a seat. *Acc. 3208.* *JB*

14 Desk and bookcase, northeastern North Carolina, 1720–35. The earliest known southern desk and bookcase, this example has the flush-hung fallboard, astragal-molded drawer and case surrounds, corbeled, or stepped, interior, well, and turned feet typical of American desks of the early eighteenth century. Few of these survive. In the Albemarle Sound region, where this piece was found, there were no towns of much consequence at the time. Nevertheless, there were artisans in the area. Living just across the sound from Edenton, then only a tiny village with sandy streets and frame houses, was Lawrence Sarson, identified as a cabinetmaker in a deed of 1714, an early use of the term. Most such tradesmen were still known as joiners during that period. His 1726 will described him as "formerly of the County of Suffolk in Great Britain . . . Cabinett Maker."

Single dovetails join the red-oak drawer frames of the large drawers of the desk. Typical of desks and bookcases of this period is the slight overhang of the bookcase at the back. Such a pragmatic feature was not inimical to the Baroque design ideal, which emphasized facades. *Acc. 2023-2.* *JB*

15

Dining table, southeastern Virginia, 1720–30. Making the transition from the gateleg table was the dropleaf dining table, which employed hinged "flies," as they were called, attached to two or more legs. The earliest examples, of which this is one, retained the oval top—here with tongue-and-groove joints at the leaves, an early feature—and the end drawer, both common to gateleg tables. The feet of this table have an unusual "hock" at the back and are carved, a feature of the earliest dropleafs, rather than lathe-turned. The gate frame is walnut, a wood commonly used in secondary positions in the Chesapeake.

Oval-top tables disappeared in the region relatively early. The new fashion was for sets of tables, two or more dining tables that could be placed together for entertaining a large party. Such tables were rectangular, but early inventories often describe them as "square." *Acc. 2024-31.*   *JB*

16

Bedstead, Pamlico area of eastern North Carolina, 1710–40. Eighteenth-century tall-post bedsteads from the Chesapeake region are rare, and this particular bed is exceptional among American examples of the period. The finely sculpted cabriole legs of all four posts are finished with the *pied de biche*, or hoof foot, favored in both France and England in the early decades of the eighteenth century; in 1749 an Elizabeth City County, Virginia, estate inventory included a black walnut table with "Colts feet." This bed is mahogany, and represents a very early use of that material in North Carolina; mahogany appears in Virginia furniture by 1730. The rails also are of mahogany, and are molded on all four edges. The sapwood exposed on the knees and footboard indicates the difficulty of obtaining high-quality imported materials. The bed has a provenance in the tiny port of Bath in Beaufort County, North Carolina's earliest town, where a significant contingent of Huguenots had settled by 1708. The relatively low height of the bed and the chamfered rather than turned posts are early details. *Acc. 2024-38.*   *JB*

17 Fireback, Tubal Furnace, Spotsylvania County, Virginia, 1725. The earliest blast furnace in America, the Falling Creek works, below the present city of Richmond, ceased to operate after the Indian massacre of 1622. It was not until almost a century later that the South resumed the production of cast iron. As early as 1717, Governor Alexander Spotswood, along with various partners including Robert Beverly, began planning the Tubal works, situated on 15,000 acres about "12 miles above the town of Fredericksburg." It was in blast by 1721, and as late as 1792 was still annually running "600 to 750 tons of Pig-iron," one of the principal products of any merchant furnace. Castings were also important. Firebacks were a common product, intended not for the reflection of heat, but to protect the brick backs of fireplaces. They often were personalized; the initials "MP" on this example were likely those of Mann Page I, who in 1725 was completing his ambitious country seat, Rosewell, on the James River. The dwelling is now a ruin. *Acc. 3956.* JB

18 Corner table, southeastern Virginia, 1750–60. The 1765 appraisal of the estate of Princess Anne County, Virginia, tavernkeeper Alexander Poole contains the entry "2 Walnut Corner Tables @ 15/." The example illustrated here, also walnut, is the product of a large school of cabinetmaking associated with Surry and Sussex counties on the south side of the James River. Characteristic of that area are the legs, which are shaped with an abrupt transition between the square upper leg stiles and the rounded portion below. Most straight legs with pad feet, a feature typical of the late Baroque style, were lathe-turned, with the leg offset in the lathe to turn the straight portion, leaving a cove, shouldered, or ogee finish just below the stiles. Corner tables were "occasional" pieces used for light meals and possibly tea service. *Acc. 2023-10.* JB

19 Side table, southeastern Virginia, 1750–80. Like the previous example, this small table is from the "southside" area of Virginia and reveals in the baluster turnings of its upper legs another strong characteristic of furniture from the Surry and Sussex area. Also typical are the large spatulate feet and the position of the drawer in a side rather than front skirt, possibly a stylistic derivation from much earlier gateleg tables. The top of this table is walnut, but the base is birch, a rare wood in Chesapeake furniture. Like many pad-foot tables made in the rural tidewater, this example is very difficult to date precisely, for the Baroque style persisted until quite late in many counties.

Mr. and Mrs. George M. Kaufman Purchase Fund, acc. 2870. JB

20 Side table, southeastern Virginia, 1750–70. A slight inward taper of the leg stiles and frame of this walnut table is an unusual detail that associates it with three other known tables from the same shop. The high, steeply coved lower portion of the feet stylistically relates the table to Williamsburg, but such features were transmitted throughout the lower tidewater and into North Carolina by emigrating journeymen. The table is finished on all four sides, and therefore could have been used for tea service and other functions suggested by the presence of a drawer.

Gift of Mrs. James Swan, acc. 3557.   JB

21 Sideboard table, attributed to Williamsburg, 1740–60. This walnut table has much the same foot pattern as the preceding table, but shows more of the urban sophistication expected of Williamsburg work. The broad knee and upper leg of this example relate the table to other examples in the MESDA files, including the earliest known cellaret. As a furniture form, the sideboard table, frequently fitted with a marble slab, was known in the seventeenth century and remained popular into the nineteenth. For example, the 1735 appraisal of the estate of Catharine Clayton of Talbot County, Maryland, listed an "old Side board Table of Black Walnut £0:10:0." Eventually the form was largely supplanted by the sideboard, a Neoclassical derivation of the 1760s that transformed the basic form of the simpler serving table by adding drawers and cabinets for storage. *Acc. 950-4.*   JB

22

Dressing table, Williamsburg, 1745–65. The skirt shaping and form of the legs of this walnut table, particularly the deeply sculpted, elongated partial scroll of the inner edges and the sharp break of the leg profile below the scroll, establish a useful stylistic signature of this shop. These details are shared by the base of a cabriole high chest attributed to the same shop, with a history of descent in the Finch family of King George County, Virginia, and now in the collection of Colonial Williamsburg. The unusual leg form of both pieces and the paneled trifid feet of the high chest suggest an Irish emigrant maker, although the Irish presence in the Chesapeake during the colonial period has not been well documented.

Cabriole-leg dressing tables, which earlier were made *en suite* with the high chests, were fashionable in Virginia and North Carolina to the end of the colonial period. This example descended in a York County family.

Gift of Mr. and Mrs. Thomas S. Douglas III, acc. 3579. JB

23

Armchair, Edenton, North Carolina, 1745–65. This chair is one of three identical mahogany armchairs, another of which also is in the MESDA collection. The affluent and highly controversial colonial agent of Lord Granville, Francis Corbin, had "8 arm mahogany chairs" worth £8:15:10 in his Edenton residence at the time of his death in 1767. The cabriole rear legs, the shaping of the crest and back stiles, the form of the arms and arm supports, and the carving style firmly link this chair with the late Baroque fashion prevalent in Britain in the 1730s. Also an early detail is the broad strapwork splat, a pattern observed on chairs from Ireland and New York; here the chairmaker failed to cross the central portion of the strap of the "figure eight" properly.

Claw feet, often taken to be Rococo or "Chippendale," are an oriental motif that appeared in Britain during the first quarter of the eighteenth century. However, they did not appear in the first edition (1754) of Chippendale's *Gentleman and Cabinet Maker's Director* and evidently were not popular in London then. The rear talons of the feet of this chair are finished with a "knife" edge, a detail not yet observed outside Edenton. The slip seat is beech, a secondary wood typical of British upholstered goods but also popular in the Chesapeake.

On loan to the museum, acc. 2418. JB

24 Desk and bookcase, eastern Maryland, 1740–50. The 1739 estate appraisal of a Captain Thornton of Calvert County, Maryland, listed a "hansom Mohogony Desk and book case" at £5. Of walnut rather than mahogany, MESDA's example has three features typical of the late Baroque style in Britain and America: arched door heads, corbeled, or stepped, interior drawers, and a well concealed under a sliding cover. Here the well opens to an upper drawer, which, like the lipped fallboard and drawers, reveals the transitional style of this piece. The beveled and wheel-cut Vauxhall glass of the bookcase was enormously expensive and is therefore rare on American case pieces. This desk and bookcase descended in the Barber family of Charles County. *Acc. 950-6.* *JB*

25 *Baltimore in 1752*, aquatint. The balance of the title includes the information "From a sketch then made by John Moale Esqr. deceased, corrected by the late Daniel Bowley Esqr." The scene was completed after 1815 with Bowley's alleged "certain recollection" along with "that of other aged persons." Although the picture no doubt suffers from a certain amount of inaccuracy, the representation of Baltimore as a mere village at the time is realistic. Some of the architectural forms are also convincing, such as the early projecting-masonry entry porch of Nicholas Rogers's house. The town was authorized in 1729, but by 1752 had no more than 200 inhabitants. Baltimore began to flourish in the late colonial period, when the Backcountry grain trade provided an exportable staple that was more lucrative than tobacco. *Acc. 2024-154.* *JB*

26

Samuel Chew, oil on canvas, by John Hesselius, Maryland, 1762. John Hesselius, son of the artist Gustavus Hesselius, was born in Philadelphia in 1728. Although Hesselius received his early training from his father, his work shows other influences from artists such as Robert Feke of Philadelphia and John Wollaston. From about 1750 to 1760, Hesselius worked in Maryland, Virginia, Delaware, and Philadelphia before settling in Annapolis. In 1762 Charles Willson Peale was one of Hesselius's pupils, exchanging a saddle for painting instruction. Hesselius died in 1778. This painting is signed "Samuel Chew/ Aetat 25/ J. Hesselius Pinx 1762."

Samuel Lloyd Chew was born in 1737 in Anne Arundel County, Maryland. He became a member of the Maryland Revolutionary Convention in 1775 and died in 1790. Hesselius's attempt to imitate Wollaston's Rococo painting technique is evident in the slanting, almond-shaped eyes and rich fabric treatment of his portrait. Characteristic of many Hesselius portraits of male subjects is the hand in the vest, which has been described as "an unreal bloated mass."

Gift of G. Wilson Douglas, Jr., acc. 2661.   FA

27

Dressing table, Norfolk, 1750–65. One of three known dressing tables from the same shop, this piece bears a remarkable resemblance to eastern Connecticut work both in general form and particularly in the style of its feet. That the maker may have emigrated from New England is also suggested by construction details such as drawers running on a single center support and drawer sides that pass the backs; neither of these details is expected in southern work of the period. Diverging from most New England work, however, and tied closely both with early New York furniture and work from the lower Chesapeake are the flush bead outlining the entire skirt and the continuous curve formed by the knee block and the line of the upper knee. The bead is a stylistic retention of the earlier cockbead. The drops are replacements but are based on originals from one of the other tables.

New England influence in the furniture of the lower Chesapeake should not be surprising in view of the amount of trade carried on between the two regions. William Byrd II caustically remarked in the late 1720s that portions of the local trade were "engrosst by the Saints of New England," and he later remarked that the "New England men" were able to "undersell you in every market." *Acc. 3929.*

JB

28 Corner chair, attributed to Peter Scott, Williamsburg, 1755–65. Details of this mahogany chair are unique in American seating furniture. The arms, rather than being joined in the center over the rear post, are interrupted by arches in the crest. The slip seat does not fit a rabbet in the frame, but instead lies atop the rails. The three rear legs are in the Chinese style. All these details are shared by another carved commode chair; an uncarved third chair of the same type has the same crest, but varies in other features.

These chairs, including the MESDA example shown here, were found in the Fredericksburg area, but the two carved chairs are clearly part of a large body of work attributed to the shop of Peter Scott (1694–1775) of Williamsburg, who had established his shop on Duke of Gloucester Street by 1733. By the 1750s Scott's custom was large enough to afford him the luxury of building an inventory, for he announced that he had on hand "sundry Pieces, of Cabinet Work, of Mahogony and Walnut, consisting of Desks, Book-Cases, Tables of various sorts," all in contrast with most early southern cabinet shops. Scott's work is distinctive in style and carving details; his claw feet are a very early form, rather elongated in profile, with heavy, softly delineated talons. *Acc. 2921.* JB

29 Tea table, attributed to Peter Scott, Williamsburg, 1755–60. Although very little is known of Scott's background, the enormous diversity of his repertoire almost certainly indicates urban British training. Despite the early date of his trade history in Virginia, he kept abreast of London styles. The most dramatic examples of Scott's work are found in three tea tables and a kettle stand. The table illustrated here and the stand utilize the same pattern of top edging, consisting of linking C- and S-scrolls interspersed with acanthus leaves, the most elaborate design used on known American tea table tops. This table is of mahogany, with a cherry pedestal. It descended from Carter Braxton (1736–97) of King William County, Virginia, a signer of the Declaration of Independence, whose manor, Elsing Green, still stands. Early records usually list "pillar and claw" or simply "round" tea tables, but the 1767 inventory of George Johnston of Fairfax County reveals another popular term of the period: "1 Moho Snap Table £1:15:00." The description obviously was derived from the spring top latch used on these tables.

Donated by Mr. and Mrs. John T. Warmath in memory of Mr. and Mrs. Henry Worsham Dew, acc. 3992. JB

30 Gaming table, Edenton, 1750–75. The knife-edged rear talons of the claw feet, among other details, closely relate this mahogany table to the Edenton armchair (23) shown earlier. Three shops in the town employed this unusual detail. One of a pair (the matching table is privately owned), this table descended from Willie Jones (1741–1802) of Halifax County, but may have been ordered originally by Jones's father, an agent of Lord Granville and attorney general of the colony. Typical of the Edenton school of cabinetmaking are the straight-shanked cabriole legs and the heavily rounded elements of the acanthus carving. Gaming tables from colonial North Carolina are very rare; in 1768 Henry McCulloh warned James Iredell, who was about to leave London for Edenton, that in his new home Iredell should "not expect the appearance of luxury and riches."
Gift of Mr. and Mrs. Thomas S. Douglas III, acc. 2720. JB

31 Writing table, Edenton, 1750–75. In 1754 an inventory of the furnishings of Eden House, a residence of Royal Governor Gabriel Johnston, listed a "Wryting" table, a form rare in America. This mahogany example is from the same shop as the preceding gaming table. It has the appearance of a dressing table but is both wider and deeper, and its upper drawer is fitted with a pen tray and ratcheted rails that once supported a reading stand. This table is straightforwardly British in form; its most unusual details are the forward-facing rear feet, often seen on the furniture of Bermuda and less frequently on coastal New England furniture made north of Boston. Such feet also appear on some British pieces.
Gift of Mr. and Mrs. James W. Douglas, acc. 3273. JB

32 Stair bracket, Edenton, 1763–65. Although specialist carvers not infrequently advertised that they would execute designs on both furniture and architecture, architectural carving by cabinetmakers is rarely found. A close comparison of carving techniques and style revealed that all the stair brackets and a large second-floor fascia for a two-story house that once stood in Edenton were carved by the same artisan who made the preceding tables. The house was built for the wealthy merchant George Blair, who purchased the lot in 1763; he died in 1769. *No accession number.* JB

33

Corner chair, attributed to Thomas White, Perquimans County, North Carolina, 1756–66. Probate inventories of the lower Chesapeake region usually describe this type of chair as a "smoking chair," and the term also was used in England. North Carolina examples with cabriole legs are very rare, but corner chairs otherwise are far more frequently encountered than armchairs. The splat pattern and form of the legs and feet place this chair in a group of furniture attributed to Thomas White (d. 1788) that consists of two dressing tables, two desks, a tall clock, and a cupboard, all walnut except for one table. Details of these pieces indicate that White almost certainly was trained in Rhode Island, although he was a native of Isle of Wight County, Virginia. He worked at the trade in Virginia before moving to Perquimans County in 1756. In 1766 he settled about forty miles west in Northampton County, where he worked until his death. This chair descended in the Cheshire family of Chowan County.

Gift of Mr. Joseph B. Cheshire, Jr., acc. 3777-1.   JB

34

Dressing table, Williamsburg, 1756–70. A large body of furniture has been attributed to the shop of Anthony Hay in Williamsburg, and this work includes that of cabinetmakers who succeeded Hay at his former establishment. Hay was working at least by 1751 and in 1756 paid £200 for two lots on Nicholson Street, where his dwelling and shop were located. In 1767 cabinetmaker Benjamin Bucktrout announced that Hay had "removed to the RAWLEIGH tavern" and that Bucktrout had "taken his shop," where he remained until 1770. This diminutive dressing table is thought to be the work of either Hay or Bucktrout. Characteristic of Williamsburg work are the form of the feet, the elegantly thin ovolo-molded top with shaped corners, and the lack of a rail above the drawers. The table is of mahogany except for the legs, which are cherry, the sort of combination seen earlier in the Scott tea table (29). *Acc. 2023-16.*   JB

35 Side chair, northeastern North Carolina, 1765–90. The most prevalent surviving statement of the Chesapeake's "neat and plain" taste is made by side chairs, most of them with splats in the George II style and bases in the Chinese taste—that is, with straight, or "Marlborough," legs. The simplest of these have a "boxed" stretcher system: the front stretcher joins the front legs rather than the side stretchers, a Chinese construction feature. Strong details of the Roanoke River basin on this walnut chair, which is one of a pair, are the relatively straight crest with a lobate profile below and the extensive use of a flush bead around all the edges of the back and splat. This extensive beading is seen from Williamsburg south into northeastern North Carolina. This example lacks a rear stretcher, an unusual feature that also occurs in a group of chairs associated with the Richmond-Petersburg area of Virginia. *Acc. 2690-1 & 2.*   *JB*

36 *Sacrifice of Isaac*, silk tent stitch on silk canvas, by Elizabeth Boush, Norfolk, 1768–69. This needlework picture, inscribed "Elizth. Boush worked this Peice at E. Gardners 1768:9," is the only such southern colonial example recorded that is known to have been made at a specific school. On 21 March 1766 Elizabeth Gardner advertised in Purdie's *Virginia Gazette* that she "had taken a house in Norfolk borough, for the accommodating young Ladies as boarders; where are taught the following things, viz. Embroidery, tent work, nuns do., queenstitch, Irish do. and all kinds of shading; also point, Dresden lace work, cat gut, &c. Shell work, wa[x] work, and artificial flowers." The subject of the needlework was probably derived from an engraving in the *Thesaurus Sacrarum Historiarum Veteris Testamenti*, published in Antwerp in 1585, an important needlework design source. Elizabeth Boush's picture of Abraham and Isaac is closely related to mid-eighteenth-century English embroideries influenced by the engravings in that volume. However, the carefully mixed colors from a variety of shaded cottons, especially in the foreground, reveal an artistic skill more often associated with Virginia work.

Elizabeth Boush was the great-granddaughter of Samuel Boush, the first Mayor of Norfolk, and the daughter of Samuel and Alice Mason Boush. She was sixteen at the time she worked this embroidery. In 1772 she married Champion Travis, and by 1797 they were living in Williamsburg. Her death date has not been recorded.

Gift of Mrs. James H. Stone, acc. 2847.   *FA*

37

Chest, Accomack County, Virginia, 1750–70. A large group of furniture from the southern portion of Virginia's Eastern Shore is characterized by extensive fields of paneling, fine architectural detail, and polychrome painted finishes. These features indicate the work of a group of skilled finish joiners working from as early as the 1730s to the end of the eighteenth century. The frames of the case pieces such as chests and wardrobes are not joined—that is, do not have facades and sides mortised-and-tenoned to the corner stiles—but instead are wainscot construction, with the ranges of paneling rabbeted at the corners and joined with nails. The blue, white, orange, and black paint of this chest is largely original. *Acc. 3331.* *JB*

38

Corner cupboard, Accomack County, 1750–60. With much the same paint scheme as the preceding chest, this small cupboard demonstrates the attention to architectural form that is typical of this group of furniture. The arched heads of the door lights, the pilasters, and the finely detailed moldings are details that would not be unusual on a paneled fireplace wall of a parlor. Corner cupboards, often called "bowfats"—a corruption of the French *buffet*—actually were an element of interior architecture until the first quarter of the eighteenth century, when free-standing cupboards came into use. Even after that time, cupboards made in coastal urban areas tended to be built into rooms rather than made as separate units. *Acc. 2989.* *JB*

39

Pair of back stools, southeastern Virginia, 1755–70. Back stools, an early form of seating furniture, were common on the Continent and in Britain in the seventeenth century. Examples from that period usually were made with turned bases and backs open just above the seat. The "4 Oak Stools with backs" listed in the 1746 estate appraisal of Peter Farmer of Baltimore County, Maryland, very likely were such examples. By the first quarter of the eighteenth century, however, back stools had evolved to a more luxuriant form. In 1772 the Charleston cabinetmaker Thomas Elfe charged John Matthews £30 for "2 back Stools"; these chairs usually were sold in pairs or sets. The mahogany examples illustrated here, the only known southern back stools, are probably the work of a Norfolk shop. The unusual stretcher piercings and fret carving of the legs are in the Chinese mode and are a design observed on British furniture. One of the chairs is upholstered in a gold silk damask, based on the original nailing on the frames. Evidence for the tufting was found in the original canvas backing. The second chair is covered with a linen check slipcover, the common method used during the period for preventing excessive wear and soil on expensive fabrics. *Acc. 3700-1 & 2.* *JB*

40

Bedstead, Halifax, North Carolina, 1774–77. Josiah Collins, one of North Carolina's most prominent merchants, was a native of Somerset, England. He arrived in the small town of Halifax in 1774 and moved down the Roanoke River to Edenton in 1777. While in Halifax he acquired this bed, which can be attributed to the Halifax cabinetmaker Richard Hall based on the style of its carving and turning. In 1765 Hall was given an order from the Royal White Hart (Masonic) Lodge in Halifax "to make a Chair for the use of the Lodge," and his carved master's chair still exists. Typical of furniture of the Roanoke River basin school, this mahogany bed uses lighter wood, here dogwood stopfluting and foot ovolos, for decorative accents. Tall-post beds were very expensive in the eighteenth century, particularly because of fabric costs. Francis Fontaine of Wilmington advertised a "high post fluted Mahogany Bedstead" in 1797. It was fitted "with cornishes," the usual finish for such beds, along with "a complete set of new Bed Curtains of fashionable yellow ground Chintz, with the fringes, lace, lines, rings leads, tassels, and pins." The price was $185.00. *Acc. 2377.* *JB*

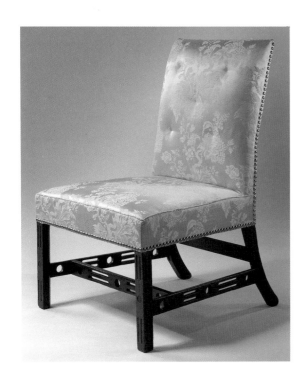

41 Cellaret, northeastern North Carolina, 1780–1800. The term "cellaret" has not been found in probate inventories in the North Carolina Albemarle. Instead, early records usually described them as "gin cases," "brandy cases," and "bottle cases," and some households had more than one. Virtually all were made to store the tapering square imported Dutch gin bottles rather than wine bottles. Although cellarets of this type—a partitioned box fitted on a frame—are common in southeastern Virginia and the Roanoke River basin of North Carolina, they are not known to have been made elsewhere in coastal America or even in Britain. This walnut example employs elm as a light wood cockbeading under the top and around the drawer, a Roanoke basin stylistic hallmark. The near-square plan of the case is typical of eighteenth-century examples. Later cellarets generally are rectangular.

   The presence of so many cellarets in the Carolina Albemarle seems to be explained by the sarcastic comments of various travelers. William Byrd II remarked in the early 1730s that "nothing is dear" in Edenton "but Law, Physick, and Strong Drink." Edenton's Dr. Brickell observed about the same time that local planters came to town and amused themselves by "drinking Rum, Punch, and other Liquors for Eight or Ten Days successively, and after they have committed this Excess, will not drink 'till such time as they take *the next Frolick*, as they call it." *Acc. 950-20.*   JB

42 Side chair, one of a pair, New Bern, North Carolina, or Norfolk, 1770–85. The back of this chair is adapted from Plate 10 of the first and second editions of Thomas Chippendale's *Gentleman and Cabinet Maker's Director*, a design source owned by several Virginia cabinetmakers but not listed in any North Carolina inventories. Nevertheless, this chair and its mate have a New Bern provenance, and the carving is related to a carved tea table that also has a Pamlico history. The 1791 inventory of New Bern architect John Hawks, the designer of the royal governor's residence, Tryon Palace, listed seventeen pieces of mahogany furniture, including chairs. The elaborate brackets of this chair are mortised into the seat frame, an unusual detail; the center stretcher is mortised through the side stretchers. Certain stylistic details suggest that this pair of chairs and other related work may have been the products of a Norfolk artisan, working either there or in New Bern.
   Mary Niven Alston Purchase Fund, acc. 3521-1 & 2.
                                                    JB

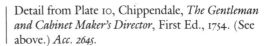

43 Detail from Plate 10, Chippendale, *The Gentleman and Cabinet Maker's Director*, First Ed., 1754. (See above.) *Acc. 2645.*

44 Armchair, northeastern North Carolina, 1750–90. The unusual combination of post-and-round and Windsor chairmaking traditions in this chair makes it difficult to date. With a history of Northampton County, this chair may represent the work of a chairmaker who had encountered sack-back Windsors imported to the region from Philadelphia. Sack-backs first appeared in the city in the early 1760s. Only one other example of such a combination of chairmaking traditions is known, a chair from the northern Shenandoah Valley of Virginia. *Acc. 3920.* JB

45

Mrs. Charles Pettigrew, pastel on paper, by William Joseph Williams, Edenton, 1785. William Joseph Williams, born in New York City in 1759, may have been the nephew of John Mare, a painter who settled in Edenton. Williams painted in a variety of places, including Edenton, Philadelphia, George-town, D.C., Charleston, New Bern, and New York, and died in New Bern in 1822. Williams's influences besides Mare are not known. His pastels indicate an aptitude for handling chalks. Blending was used to create highlights and light from the upper right to produce shadows. The blue coloring noticeable in the background of this portrait is unusual but compliments Mrs. Pettigrew's dress, throws her face lines into relief, and adds dimension to the pastel.

Mrs. Pettigrew, née Mary Blount, was the wife of Reverend Charles Pettigrew, the first bishop-elect of the Episcopal Diocese in North Carolina. She died in 1786, after moving from Edenton to Harvey's Neck. Williams did portraits of both Pettigrews; the Reverend's is also in the MESDA collection. This portrait is signed "Wm. Williams Pinxit/ Edenton, Sept. 15th 1785."

J. M. Robinson Purchase Fund, acc. 3332.　　　*FA*

46

Silver sauceboat, marked "I M," Norfolk, 1765–75. This sauceboat is one of a pair decorated with serrated lines and punchwork. It has cast scroll handles and three cast flared pad feet. It is stamped "I M" three times; the mark has been attributed to James Murphree, who worked in Norfolk from about 1754 to 1775 and in Southampton County, Virginia, from 1775 until his death in 1782. The form of the cut- and punchwork border on the upper edge of this piece is unusual, although similar types of borders have been seen on Boston silver of about the same period. The bottom of the sauceboat is engraved with the initials of its original owners, James and Molly Murdaugh, who were married in Princess Anne County, Virginia, on 20 February 1764.

On loan to the museum, acc. 2814.　　　*FA*

47 Officer's hanger (1785–95), by William and George Richardson, with breastplate (1812), Richmond. Silver-mounted swords made in the South are rare, although southern silversmiths advertised them regularly. The "W & GR" touch on this hanger, or officer's sword, is that of the Richardson brothers, who worked·in partnership from before 1782 until 1798, when their shop was destroyed by fire. William Richardson continued in the trade until his death in 1809. His estate contained a "quantity of Silversmith's Tools and Sweepings." The unmarked silver breastplate bears the inscription "7th USR," a regiment formed at the time of the War of 1812. The hanger, scabbard, strap, and breastplate descended from William Jones (1764–1847) of Gloucester County, an officer during the War of 1812.

Donated by Sarah S. Rogers, Mrs. L. Dobbs Bellinger, Mrs. Vernet O. Stark, and Mrs. B. L. Williams in memory of Powell Burwell Rogers, acc. 2909.　　　JB

48 *Unknown Soldier*, watercolor on ivory miniature, by Lawrence Sully, Richmond or Norfolk, 1800–1802. Lawrence Sully, the older brother of the artist Thomas Sully and the cabinetmaker Chester Sully, was born in Kilkenny, Ireland, in 1769. He and his brothers emigrated to America in 1792 with their parents, both actors. Sully established himself as a miniaturist and fancy painter in Richmond, except for a brief residence in Norfolk from 1801 to 1802, executing mourning devices and hairwork. He died in 1804 from injuries received in a brawl with some drunken sailors.

Sully was one of Thomas Sully's earliest instructors, for at the age of sixteen, in 1799, Thomas left Charleston and the auspices of a miniaturist named Belzon to live and study with his brother. Although there are slight resemblances between the Sullys' works, Thomas clearly was the more skilled, and his works soon surpassed his brother's. *Acc. 2032-1.*　　　FA

49   *Mrs. George Grundy*, oil on canvas, by Charles Willson Peale, Baltimore, 1789. Charles Willson Peale, one of the founding fathers of American art, was born in Queen Anne's County, Maryland, in 1741. When Charles was nine his family moved to Annapolis, where he was apprenticed to a saddler. Peale developed an interest in painting during a visit to Norfolk in the 1760s. Returning to Annapolis, he took lessons from John Hesselius and began painting portraits. By 1767 he had acquired a patron and enough subscriptions for a trip to London to study with Benjamin West and Alan Ramsey. He moved to Philadelphia in 1775 and served in the Pennsylvania militia during the Revolutionary War. He painted miniatures of many of Washington's officers, and in 1779 he was commissioned by the Executive Council of Pennsylvania to paint a portrait of Washington for their chambers. After the Revolution, his career was mainly centered in Philadelphia. He died in 1827.

Mrs. Grundy, née Mary Carr, was born in 1762. She married the merchant George Grundy in 1780 and lived with him at their estate, Bolton, near Baltimore, until her death in 1796. The child in the portrait was her daughter Mary, born in April 1788. Their portrait was completed in January 1789, and on 24 January 1789 Peale wrote in his diary: "Mrs. Grundy and child I believe quite done, this picture I esteem one of my best pieces—the mother being a fine figure and the child handsome." Two days later, however, he added "I painted anew the head of Mrs. Grundy which pleased better than the first."

The portrait, signed by the painter, reveals several features typical of Peale's work. The faces are oval-shaped; Mrs. Grundy's hair is piled high, is laced with a ribbon, and falls into a long curl with wispy treatment; her head is tilted slightly to the left and is balanced by the child. The sash ending in a gold tassel at Mrs. Grundy's waist and the red upholstered chair with gilt carving are also Peale characteristics. Peale's influence on his nephew Charles Peale Polk is obvious when this painting is compared with Polk's portrait (50) of Mrs. Riddell and her daughter Agnes. *Acc. 3973.*   *FA*

50 *Mrs. Robert Riddell*, oil on canvas, by Charles Peale Polk, Baltimore, 1791. Charles Peale Polk, the nephew of Charles Willson Peale and the son of Robert and Elizabeth Digby Peale Polk, was born in 1767. His mother died in 1773, and by 1776 he was living in his uncle's household. In 1778 Peale began instructing Polk in the methods and techniques of drawing and painting. Polk never quite achieved his uncle's prosperity, although he painted portraits of such influential figures as George Washington, Thomas Jefferson, and James Madison. He was constantly in debt and often had to pursue other occupations to keep afloat financially. From 1785 to 1801, Polk worked in Philadelphia,

Baltimore, western Virginia, and northern Maryland. By 1802 he was a government clerk in Washington, a position he held until 1819. He died in 1822.

Mrs. Robert Riddell, born Mary Hawksworth in 1761, died in 1806. Riddell was a Baltimore merchant. Their daughter Agnes, who was probably about five years old at the time the portrait was painted, married Kennedy Owen in December 1806. Peale's influence on his nephew's work is particularly evident in the oval shapes of the sitters' faces, Mrs. Riddell's elegant costume accessories, the treatment of her hair, her pose, and the chair in which she is seated. *Acc. 3374.*   *FA*

51 Appliquéd bedspread, Gloucester County, Virginia, and Warren County, North Carolina, late eighteenth century. This bedspread is one of the earliest southern-made textiles in the MESDA collection. Two French copperplates and three English block prints were used for the appliqué, applied with a reverse buttonhole stitch; these materials date about 1785. The blue calico bands probably date about 1800. The bedspread descended in the Hayes family of Gloucester County, Virginia, and Warren County, North Carolina, and was made by Sarah Willis Hayes, the wife of Willis Hayes. According to family history, Mrs. Hayes began making the coverlet in Virginia in the late 1700s but did not finish it until after she had moved to North Carolina.

Donated by Mrs. Elmo D. Sparks in memory of Sarah Elizabeth Burwell, acc. 2669. FA

52 Corner cupboard, northeastern North Carolina, 1790–1800. One of over twenty-eight known pieces produced by one shop in the Roanoke River basin school of cabinetmaking, this walnut cupboard has a tympanum inset with a roundel bearing the initials "WH," as do five other pieces from the same shop. These initials, inlaid with what appears to be gesso, might be those of the cabinetmaker. The earliest piece from this shop, a Franco-German style blockfront desk by the same artisan, suggests that he may have been a deserter from the Regiment von Bose, which in 1781 marched through Hertford and Northampton counties with Lord Cornwallis. Stylistic signatures of this shop are the flamelike pierced finial, the whirling-star rosette inlays fitted with turned bone "buttons" in their centers, the low-relief ebonized leaf-and-vine carving of the tympanum, and the profile of the feet. The shaped heads of the upper lights of the doors precisely match the blocking plan of the French-style desk. The blind, or paneled, lower lights are typical of cupboards and presses in the North Carolina Albemarle. With a history of descent in the Cotten family of Hertford County, this cupboard is one of a pair; its mate is privately owned. *Acc. 906.* *JB*

53 Corner cupboard, Norfolk, 1790–1800. This piece is one of the few surviving corner cupboards made in the urban coastal South. Its formality and its cross-banded mahogany veneers lend it a strongly British aspect. Several other cupboards with similar details have been seen, all very likely the work of a Norfolk shop. In contrast, no free-standing Neoclassical cupboards from Baltimore or Charleston have been recorded. Characteristic of Norfolk work is the use of a black pitchlike material for inlay instead of ebony. On this cupboard, the dark portion of the door stringing is pitch, which is a logical substitute for wood in a port city noted for its shipbuilding. *Acc. 3931.* *JB*

54

Secretary, Norfolk, 1790–1805. The horizontal stringing and husks, or "bellflowers," of the frieze of the preceding corner cupboard are repeated on this mahogany secretary. Here the frieze inlay is particularly related to Neoclassical case furniture made in Salem, Massachusetts, which is not surprising since large quantities of venture furniture were sent South from Salem. The letter compartments under the interior drawers are another New England detail not usual in Virginia work. This secretary descended from Robert Barraud Taylor of Norfolk, a wealthy merchant and distinguished jurist. He was a member of the grand jury that indicted Aaron Burr for treason in 1807, and during the War of 1812 he commanded a militia that defeated a superior force of 4,000 British troops attacking Norfolk. *Acc. 3807.*   *JB*

55

Side chair, Norfolk, 1790–1800. The particularly colorful inlay on the back of this mahogany chair relates it to three others with Virginia histories. All have the same unusual pendant leg inlay, which incorporates pitch for the dark elements. Also unusual is the pattern of swagged upholstery nails, which here duplicates evidence on the chair rail. Such decorative nailing normally does not include a top row of nails. The seat is covered in a replica patterned horsehair, a favored Neoclassical seating material. A 1795 oil portrait of Elizabeth Hack Henry of Accomack County, Virginia, depicts the sitter in a chair of this design. *Acc. 3908.*   *JB*

56 Armchair, by James Woodward, Norfolk, 1803. This mahogany chair is one of the "12 Mahogany Chairs at 10 Dol. Each . . . $120.00" billed to General John Hartwell Cocke by the Norfolk cabinetmaker James Woodward on 18 June 1803. Woodward first advertised in Norfolk in 1793, seeking journeymen cabinetmakers. In 1795 he announced that he had "the best Workmen of Philadelphia and New-York, and from Europe," and noted that he had on hand "Chairs, Sideboards, sets of Card, Pier, Pembroke, Tea, Dining Tables, elegant Sophas, Ladies Dressing Tables, mahogany 4 post Bedsteads, Clock Cases." By 1813 he had opened a wareroom in Richmond as well, and in 1815 he was listed as a director of the Bank of Virginia. His large inventory on hand normally would suggest that Woodward imported northern furniture as well as producing his own work, but his establishment was so large that he may indeed have been able to make furniture for display, something few southern cabinetmakers could do. The style of this armchair recalls his mention of "the best Workmen of . . . New-York," for the chair is closely related to seating furniture made in that city. Other work that can be documented to Woodward, including a breakfast table in the MESDA collection, is more vernacular in nature.

Loaned by the Dallas Museum of Art, acc. 4014. JB

57 Pembroke table, Norfolk, 1790–1800. The term Pembroke, designating an "occasional" or "breakfast" table, was in use in Britain by the 1760s, although the basic form was earlier. The most common American Neoclassical forms of these tables have four fixed legs, with the leaves supported by a pair of short gates, or "flies," hinged to the outer frame. They are often difficult to attribute to a specific region, but the origin of this example is clear. The incised husks trailing from a pendant of stringing on the legs, in addition to the dot-and-lenticular inlays below, show the influence of Salem, Massachusetts, but the panels in the leg stiles are ornamented with lunetted borders and quatrefoil inlays executed with the pitchlike material that are typical of Norfolk work. The same inlay has been observed on a large group of furniture attributable to the city.

Gift of Mr. and Mrs. Cleve G. Harris, acc. 3639. JB

Mary Poythress Epes Doswell, tempera on ivory miniature, attributed to Francis Rabineau, Nottoway County, Virginia, 1802. The attribution of this miniature to Francis Rabineau is based on signed examples of his work. Rabineau was an itinerant miniaturist and crayon portraitist who was first recorded in New York in 1791. From 1795 to 1796 he worked in New Jersey, where he also painted standards and colors for the New Jersey militia regiments. In 1797 he was advertising in New Bern as a "LIMNER, FROM PHILADELPHIA," in 1798 he was in Wilmington and Fayetteville, North Carolina, in 1802 he was working in Richmond, and in 1804 he had moved to Lynchburg. An estate notice in the Richmond *Enquirer* of 16 January 1808 indicates that he probably died in Richmond in late 1807 or early 1808.

Mary Poythress Epes Doswell of Nottoway County, Virginia, was the wife of Major John Doswell and the mother of Mary Elizabeth Poythress Doswell, whose needlework picture (59) is also in the MESDA collection.

Gift of Mrs. T. Randolph Perkinson, acc. 3187-1.   FA

 59   Needlework picture, silk on linen, by Mary Elizabeth Poythress Doswell, Nottoway County, 1802. Mary Elizabeth Poythress Doswell was the daughter of Mary Poythress Epes Doswell and Major John Doswell of Nottoway County. A miniature (58) of Mrs. Doswell attributed to Francis Rabineau is in the MESDA collection, as is a mourning miniature of P. E. Doswell, her son and Mary Elizabeth's brother.

Like the Boush and Stetson needlework pieces (36, 60), this silk-on-linen embroidery (left), inscribed "Mary Elizabeth Poythress Doswell Taught by Mrs./ Woodson Finished This Piece July 1802 in the 11 Year/ of her age," represents a very important part of a young southern girl's education. Ornamental needle arts were among the accomplishments deemed necessary for young women in England and America, particularly those in the upper classes. According to Thomas Woody's *A History of Women's Education in the United States*, one of Thomas Jefferson's descendants wrote of women's education on the southern plantation: "Very little from books was thought necessary for a girl. She was trained to domestic matters . . . to play upon the harpsichord or spinet, and to work impossible dragons and roses on canvas."

Nothing is known of Mrs. Woodson. She probably was a schoolteacher in Nottoway County.

Gift of Mrs. T. Randolph Perkinson, acc. 3187-3.   FA

60   Needlework embroidery, chenille on silk, by Mary Ann Stetson, Richmond, 1818. On 22 September 1817, Miss Euphania Ferguson, formerly the "Preceptress, in the Hertford Academy" in Murfreesboro, North Carolina, announced that she was opening an "Institution for the tuition of young Ladies, in all the polite and necessary branches of Female Education" in Richmond. Among the subjects she offered were "Embroidery" and "Plain and Ornamental Needle work." In another advertisement she stated that her school was located on "Shockoe Hill, corner of 11 and 10th streets" and listed her terms for various subjects, which included five dollars per quarter for plain and ornamental needlework.

This chenille-on-silk embroidery (above) of a basket of flowers probably was an exercise in ornamental needlework at Miss Ferguson's school. It is signed in ink: "Mary Ann Stetson, Richmond, 20 July 1818, Euphania Ferguson's Seminary." Benjamin Stetson, a Richmond merchant, married Nancy Lyle on 30 March 1805; perhaps they were Mary Ann's parents. *Acc. 3569.*   FA

61

Lamb Family, oil on canvas, attributed to Henry Benbridge, Norfolk, 1800–1802. This portrait (right) of Margaret Stuart and William Boswell Lamb and their daughter Martha Anne, along with another in the MESDA collection, that of the Francis Stubbs Taylor family, is not signed but has been attributed to Henry Benbridge based on the classical setting, subjects' poses, and slightly disproportionate figures. Both family portraits are the only examples of conversation pieces known to have been painted in Norfolk in the early nineteenth century, and they were the first to be attributed to Benbridge's Norfolk period. Benbridge was a well-known Charleston artist for over twenty years (36, 37 Low Country). After leaving Charleston for health reasons sometime in the 1790s, Benbridge settled in Norfolk, where he was first recorded about 1800. About 1801 he met Thomas Sully, who had been studying with his brother Lawrence Sully; according to tradition, it was Benbridge's work in oils that inspired Sully to try that medium. Benbridge left Norfolk after 1810 and eventually moved to Philadelphia, where he died in 1813.

William Boswell Lamb was a Norfolk merchant who served as mayor of that city for several terms between 1810 and 1823. About 1805 Lamb had an office on Main Street; also on Main Street was the Norfolk Hotel, which was operated by Benbridge's son Harry from 1804 to 1806. It is also thought that the James Boswell who commissioned Benbridge's painting of Paoli in Corsica was related to Lamb.

Gift of Mr. and Mrs. Alban K. Barrus, acc. 2943.

FA

62

Mr. Benjamin Yoe and Son and *Mrs. Benjamin Yoe and Daughter*, oil on canvas, by Joshua Johnson, Baltimore, 1810–12. Joshua Johnson, the earliest recorded southern black artist, was listed as a portrait painter and limner in various Baltimore city directories from 1796 to 1824. In the 1817 directory his name appeared in the listings for "Free Householders of Colour," indicating that he was a free black. In 1802 he advertised in the Baltimore *Telegraphe and Daily Advertiser*; this appears to have been his only notice. Nothing more is known of his

life. His painting style is stiff, the arms and hands particularly rigid; his faces are three-quarters full, and the mouths of his sitters are drawn in tightly. Although his style is certainly more primitive than that of Charles Peale Polk, his rigid manner suggests that he was influenced by Polk.

Benjamin Yoe was a Baltimore tailor; his wife was born Susannah Amos. Their children were Benjamin Franklin, born in 1804, and Mary Elizabeth, born in 1806.

Gift of John W. Hanes, acc. 2170-1 & 2.　　　*FA*

63 *Robert Rankin*, charcoal on paper, by Charles Balthazar Julien Fevret de Saint-Mémin, Baltimore, 1804–9. Charles Saint-Mémin and his family fled to Switzerland from France during the French Revolution and then emigrated to America in 1793. He worked in Baltimore, Richmond, Charleston, and Washington before returning to France in 1814. He died there in 1852.

Saint-Mémin used a physiognotrace, a rectangular frame that slid vertically between two upright pieces of wood to which were attached a movable magnifying glass and a projecting arm holding a pencil, to take accurate, life-size profiles. Many early-nineteenth-century portraitists were interested in this form of cutting profiles. Charles Willson Peale and his sons not only built their own machine, but developed another with Thomas Jefferson that could make more than one copy at once.

The faint coloring on this painting was created with pink gouache. Opaque colors were ground in water and mixed with gum and water to create a paste used in both profile drawing and miniature painting. Rankin's uniform in this portrait is that of a lieutenant in the Marine Corps. *Acc. 1044.*   FA

64 Pier table, Baltimore, 1801–2. Thomas Sheraton defined pier tables as tables "made to fit in between the architraves of the windows, and rise above the surbase." This mahogany, poplar, and white pine Neoclassical example with satinwood, poplar, and ebony inlays fits Sheraton's description and exhibits ornamentation generally associated with Baltimore work, particularly the reverse painted glass panels and the three-part bellflowers with elongated center petals. The shape of this table is illustrated in *The London Cabinet Makers' Union Book of Prices* with the suggestion that it can be fitted with two or three legs at the end. The back overhang of its top follows George Hepplewhite's recommendation that when pier tables rise above "the dado of the room, nearly touching the elements of the glass . . . the top [should fit] close to the wall."

The name Kennedy is scratched on the center panel of the table and printed on the waistbands of the figures on the center legs. The panels have therefore been attributed to Samuel Kennedy, a carver and gilder who advertised in the Baltimore *American and Daily Advertiser* in 1801 that he was from Philadelphia. Among his services he listed "Ornamental carving and gilding . . . Brackets, Window Cornices, Gold Letters on Glass, &c." The table originally was one of a pair that stood in Mount Vernon.

Loaned by the Kaufman Americana Foundation, acc. 3018-2.   FA

65 Tall clock, works by William Elvins, Baltimore, 1800–1810. Between 1706 and 1816, William Elvins worked at four different addresses in the Fells Point section of Baltimore. The mahogany case that houses his eight-day movement is a strong statement of the Baltimore Neoclassical style, particularly the grapevine and husk inlay of the hood but including the compass-drawn stringing below the hood and the spandrel inlays of the waist door. The pierced scroll-and-leaf tracery forming the tympanum of this clock is a reconstruction based on another clock case attributed to the same cabinetmaker. Tall clocks were made in profusion in Baltimore after the Revolution, and the clockmakers readily procured cases from among the over seventy cabinetmakers working in the city by 1810. Although heavily influenced by the Philadelphia style earlier, during the Neoclassical period Baltimore developed a strong regional style of its own. *Acc. 2651.* JB

66 Pembroke table, attributed to the shop of John Shaw, Annapolis, Maryland, 1790–95. Of mahogany, oak, yellow pine, and sweet gum with light wood inlay, this Neoclassical Pembroke table has been attributed to the shop of John Shaw, Annapolis's preeminent cabinetmaker in the late eighteenth century. Over fifty pieces of furniture labeled by Shaw have been recorded, and many others have been attributed to his shop. Typical of Shaw's work, as demonstrated by this example, are the type of applied molding at the frame base, the shape of the top and the use of thin wood for its construction, the double gate, the ovoid spade feet, and the light wood cockbeading on the drawer. The trifid terminals of the stringing and the quatrefoil motifs on the feet and upper legs are also considered Shaw characteristics. At least nine other similar tables, some plain and some ornamented with variations of these inlay patterns, have been documented, but this table is considered one of Shaw's most sophisticated pieces.

Shaw was born in Scotland in 1745. He was first recorded in Annapolis in 1763. From 1772 to 1775 he worked in partnership with fellow cabinetmaker Archibald Chisolm, and during the Revolution he was appointed Armorer for the State of Maryland. Much of his work was commissioned by the Maryland government, including furniture for the State House, the Chancery Office, the Land Office, and the Orphans Court. He died in 1829.

This table is inscribed "Mary Shaws Table" on the drawer interior and probably was made for Shaw's older daughter, Mary, who lived with her father until his death.

Loaned by the Kaufman Americana Foundation, acc. 3125. FA

67 Pair of pocket pistols, attributed to John or William Bullard, Fredericksburg, Virginia, 1800–1815. Very little is known of John Bullard, who appears to have been an emigrant English gunmaker. A fowling piece dated 1799 and two rifles, one bearing his signature, have been found. The rifles date from the Revolutionary period, and one of them is much in the style of an English fowler of the period. With the exception of the scroll at the inside rear of the trigger guards, the pistols illustrated here are straightforwardly British in style; the French influence on British work is seen in the checkering pattern of the walnut grips. Simply signed "Bullard," these are the only known pair of American flintlock pocket pistols. Another Fredericksburg gunmaker, William Bullard, very likely was related and could have been the maker of these diminutive defense weapons. In 1829 he purchased, among other things, "2 lots lock filing Tools" for $6.00 from the estate of Madison Davis; William Bullard's own 1831 inventory indicates that he was still working at the time of his death.

Gift of Thomas S. Douglass III, acc. 3176-1 & 2.   JB

68 Copper kettle, attributed to James Kelly, Baltimore, 1820–30. The existence of this pot, which is stamped on its handle "J. KELLY/ BALTIMORE," suggests that at least one Baltimore apprentice completed his indenture and opened his own establishment. In January 1819 the proceedings of the Baltimore Orphans Court included this entry: "James Kelly an Orphan boy of the age of Sixteen years the Seventeenth day of March next is bound unto Hugh Allen to be taught the trade of a Coppersmith." Thousands of apprentices were taken to early trades; few appear in the records following their indenture. Southern copperware is rare, and signed examples almost invariably are the products of urban shops.

Gift of Thomas A. Gray, acc. 2695.   JB

69 Silver bowl, by John Gaither, Alexandria, Virginia, 1807–12. This ten-inch footed punchbowl, weighing over forty-two ounces, is the largest such southern bowl recorded. It descended in the Marsteller family of Alexandria. John Gaither was in partnership with silversmith Greenberry Griffith from 1807 until 1812, when Gaither moved to Washington. The partnership was an unusual one, for it was listed in tax assessments as "Gaither & Griffith, retail merchants." The firm advertised "a general assortment of Gold and Silver Watches" along with other silver objects. This may have been imported work, which would account for the "retail" aspect. During this period, however, Gaither also advertised under his own name at the "Corner of Prince and Fairfax Streets." After his move to the capital, Gaither continued to work until 1817. *Acc. 3465.*   JB

70 Silver service, by C. A. Burnett, Georgetown, D.C., 1815–20. Charles A. Burnett was in partnership with Thomas Rigden as early as 1801. By 1806 he operated his own establishment, where, as he noted in one advertisement, he sold watches, jewelry, flatware, and other articles imported from London and Liverpool as well as made "gold and silver ware, at the most reduced prices." Burnett was a prolific and successful silversmith. The five-piece service shown here descended in the Loughborough family of Washington. The increasingly eclectic styles of late Neoclassical silver required a radical shift in technology, causing many southern silversmiths to import virtually everything except for flatware. New York and Philadelphia firms made quantities of hollow ware for southern silversmiths and often supplied castings or elaborate rolled banding such as the friezes adorning the upper bodies and feet of this service and the gadrooned borders of the rims. Burnett certainly imported these elements for this service, but the actual raising of each piece, with the difficult repoussé lobing of the bodies, appears to be the work of Burnett's shop.

Donated by Marian I. Donovan in memory of James P. Donovan, acc. 3307-1 to 5. JB

71 Apothecary cabinet, Maryland, 1785–95. This small mahogany and poplar cabinet with mahogany veneers and a light wood inlay band is arranged so that small cubicles designed for bottles are revealed and two hinged compartments open when the lid is lifted. The hinged compartments make up one-half the depth of the cabinet and face the cabinet rear, which also has a number of small drawers, when it is closed. The cabinet is supported on ogee bracket feet.

Apothecary cabinets—also called physics chests, traveling doctor's shops, and family medicine chests—were used by both physicians and families. In the South, particularly on plantations, responsibility for nursing and healing the sick was one of the many duties assigned to the women of the house. For example, while visiting the Byrds at Westover in Virginia, the Marquis de Chastellux wrote that Mrs. Byrd "takes great care of her [slaves], makes them as happy as their situation will admit, and serves them herself as a doctor in time of sickness." Not many of these cabinets have survived. A Pennsylvania chest of about the same period as this example is in the Mabel Brady Garvan Collection at Yale University, and a later chest descending in the Dandridge-Payne families of Virginia was featured in an article in the April 1950 issue of *Antiques*. The MESDA cabinet and the Yale chest operate similarly but are not alike in design.

This example descended in a Frederick, Maryland, family and is believed to have been used on a plantation rather than in a doctor's office. Although it probably was made more than twenty years after the publication of the third edition of Chippendale's *Director* (1762), its drawer configuration and basic design are related to the cabinet illustrated in plate 120 of that work. *Acc. 2217.* FA

72 Gold medallion engraved on the reverse "C. Pryce Fecit J. Sands Sc.," Baltimore, 1824. This gold medallion is a lost-wax casting brazed to a sheet-gold back. It was presented to General Lafayette on 11 October 1824 during his visit to Baltimore in the course of his Farewell Tour. Part of the inscription on the reverse reads "Presented to Genl. Lafayette . . . in behalf of the Young Men of Baltimore." The front is stamped "OUR GRATITUDE OCTOBER 19th 1783." Lafayette's visit to the United States during 1824 and 1825 sparked a revival of patriotic fervor. The eagle perched atop the globe on this medallion, although a popular motif of the American Neoclassical style, is also a manifestation of this rekindled patriotism.

At the time he made the medal, Charles Pryse was employed at Samuel Kirk's factory in Baltimore. Sometime after the medal was presented, Pryse moved to Washington, D.C., where he advertised in 1834 that he was "the ONLY MANUFACTURER of Silver Plate in this District." J. Sands, who was responsible for the inscription on the medal, was listed as an "engraver and copper plate printer" in the Baltimore City Directory for 1824; nothing else is known about him.

It is possible that Pryse's medal was influenced by that of the Society of the Cincinnati, which features an American eagle bearing a shield. However, Pryse's design, although it has some of the same features, appears to be original. *Acc. 2380.*

FA

73 *Mistippee,* oil on canvas, by Charles Bird King, Washington, D.C., 1825. Charles Bird King was born in Newport, Rhode Island, in 1785 and attended school with Washington Allston. Allston and the miniaturist Edward Malbone, both from Newport, encouraged King's interest in painting, and in 1800 he began studying with Edward Savage, a New York artist. In 1806 he traveled to London, where he studied at the Royal Academy with Benjamin West. Among his American acquaintances also training under West were Thomas Sully, Allston, Samuel F. B. Morse, and Robert Leslie. King returned to the United States in 1812 and worked in Philadelphia, Richmond, and Baltimore before settling in Washington in 1819. He died there in 1862. Although probably best known for his Indian portraits, most of which were commissioned by the Department of War from 1821 to 1842, King also painted portraits and still life arrangements.

Mistippee accompanied his father to Washington in 1825. Named Benjamin by his parents, he was often called Ben or Benny out of respect for his family, and "Mr. Ben" eventually became Mistiben and finally "Mistippee." In this portrait (right), inscribed "Mistipe, Yoholo-Mico's son, Creek Indian. C. B. King, Washington, 1825," he is posed in a manner that can be traced back to Gainsborough and the English Rococo.

Gift of Mr. and Mrs. James Douglas, acc. 3542. *FA*

Breakfast table, by Gustavus Beall, Georgetown, D.C., or New York City, 1811–16. The straightforward New York style of this table, including the shaping of the leaves, the form of the pedestal, and the carving style, is the result of Beall's own trade background. New York City directories list him there in 1811 and 1812. The 1811-dated label pasted under the cross-batten of this table appears to be an offprint from an advertisement, since it notes that Beall had "taken the Stand lately occupied by WORTHINGTON AND BEALL in High-street, Georgetown" and had "received a large supply of the best materials from New-York, and employed good and faithful workmen." The "Worthington" must have been William Worthington, Jr., who is known to have worked in the District of Columbia from 1802 until 1822. He advertised in 1811 that he had "removed his cabinet shop from High Street in George Town, to his shop . . . in the City of Washington."

That date appears to signal the termination of the partnership of Worthington and Beall, so Beall could have produced this table in either New York or Georgetown. He was still listed in New York City directories in 1812, but such directory entries were often out of date. The white pine and oak secondary woods of this table do not solve the

puzzle, since white pine was used extensively by southern cabinetmakers during the Neoclassical period. It is evident that Beall, like many urban southern cabinetmakers, warehoused furniture of his own make as well as furniture made by others; he may have had such an arrangement with Worthington even before he left New York. In any event, Beall "removed his Cabinet and Upholstering Warehouse to the west side of High St. (nearly opposite his former Store)" in 1816 and continued to operate in the city until at least 1820, branching into various other businesses including land speculation. *Acc. 2556.* *JB*

75 Stoneware storage jar, marked by Benjamin DuVal, Richmond, 1811–17. Benjamin DuVal was working at the pottery trade in Richmond as early as 1791, when he advertised for a journeyman "who understands working at the wheel." Not until 1811, however, did DuVal announce that he had "commenced a *STONE WARE* MANUFACTORY." In 1812 another notice observed that stoneware by "*B. Duval & Co.*" would be sold at "the New-York wholesale prices." That was a significant statement, for large quantities of salt-glazed stoneware were shipped south in the venture trade from New York, beginning in the eighteenth century and continuing well into the nineteenth. It would have been difficult for a small pottery such as DuVal's to compete with large firms such as the Crolius works in New York. DuVal turned the operation of the "Richmond Stone Ware Manufactory" over to his son James in 1817, possibly terminating the use of the "B. DuVal & Co./ Richmond" mark found on this jar.

Gift of Mrs. Robert Hopper, acc. 2950.   *JB*

76 Windsor bench, Mecklenburg County, Virginia, 1780–1800. Made of poplar, hickory, and yellow pine, this low-backed bench is the earliest known example of Windsor furniture from Virginia. The bench was part of the original furnishings of Prestwould, a fine seven-bay late Palladian stone manor built in the early 1790s by Sir Peyton and Lady Jean Skipwith, residents of Virginia well before the house was completed. The stylish base and well-sculpted seat are of urban quality, although the turnings of the arm supports and the chunky termination of the arms suggest a rural chairmaker. Advertisements indicate that such benches were largely intended for passage and porch use. This example originally was painted red, and that color has been restored.

Gift of Mr. and Mrs. Frank Borden Hanes, Sr., acc. 3840.   *JB*

77 Windsor writing-arm chair, by Andrew and Robert McKim, Richmond, 1802. Owing to the specialized nature of Windsor chair manufacture and the very extensive exportation of Windsor furniture from Philadelphia and New York, few southern cities were known for the production of such chairs. One city that did support an extensive chairmaking trade was Richmond. This writing-arm chair—a form rare in the South—bears a label with the inked date "May 31st 1802" that reads: "WINDSOR CHAIRS/ Made, Warranted and Sold by/ ANDREW & ROBT. M'KIM/ At their Shop just below the Capitol/ RICHMOND." The McKim brothers carried on their chairmaking partnership at the corner of Main and 10th streets from 1795 until 1805, when Andrew McKim died. This chair shows a certain amount of Philadelphia influence. The rake of its legs is extreme, presumably for greater stability. The dark green paint—the most popular color for American Windsors—has been restored.

Gift of Mrs. Lola Harris and Mr. and Mrs. Cleve Harris, acc. 3182.   JB

78 Set of Windsor chairs, by William Pointer, Richmond, 1800–1805. William Pointer appears in the 1782 census of Richmond, and by 1796 he was in partnership with Joseph Childres. The partners announced that they had "commenced business on Shockoe Hill" and had on hand "a large assortment of the best finished WINDSOR CHAIRS." In 1808 Pointer's obituary reported that he was a "worthy man, and a respectable mechanic"; he evidently was successful in his trade. The 1809 sale of his estate listed purchases of over twenty-three dozen chairs that were sold, certainly a "large assortment." Another chairmaker, Robert McKim, bought one lot of "verdegreese" (verdigris) for making green paint, along with "one lot chair bows" and "one lot turned timber," together worth $19, indicating that Pointer's shop was still quite productive. MESDA's set of Pointer chairs consists of four side chairs and two armchairs, all originally painted green. They bear Pointer's label, which locates his shop "between Crouch's Tavern and The Governor's House." The use of continuous-arm construction is rare on Windsor armchairs made south of New York City, but it appears to have been common in Richmond. *Acc. 1141-1 to 6.*   JB

79 Settee, Baltimore, 1805–10. Made of poplar, this red and gold painted and decorated bow-front settee with a cane seat has a walnut seat frame characteristic of Baltimore fancy furniture. Four painted panels adorn the top rail of the back, and musical instruments have been painted on the four front rails. Although japanned furniture was being made in Philadelphia and New York in the early nineteenth century, Baltimore fancy furniture makers produced it on a scale and with style unequaled by any other major cabinetmaking center. They also exported their work as far as Charleston, Savannah, and the West Indies. During the first decades of the nineteenth century, Baltimore chairmakers and painters such as John and Hugh Finlay based their work on classical designs from the drawing books of Sheraton and Hepplewhite, for painted furniture had gained popularity in England in the last dec-

ades of the eighteenth century. Sheraton's 1803 *Cabinet Dictionary* even included instructions for painting and drawing lines on chairs. The Baltimore furniture painters followed the techniques outlined by Sheraton, applying polychrome and gilt decoration freehand over a colored ground with a lavish use of varnish.

In 1805 the Finlays advertised that they made "CANE SEAT CHAIRS, SOFAS, RECESS, and WINDOW SEATS of every description and all colors, gilt, ornamented and varnished in a stile not equalled on the continent—with real Views, Fancy Landscapes, Flowers, Trophies of Music, War, Husbandry, Love, &c. &c." This settee has not been attributed to the Finlays, but it fits their description with its "Fancy Landscapes" and "Trophies of Music" and probably was made about the same time as the notice was published. *Acc. 1124.*

FA

THE LOW COUNTRY

The Low Country

Like the Chesapeake, but perhaps even to a greater degree, the South Carolina Low Country was closely aligned with British culture and ideals. In 1740 Eliza Lucas of Charleston wrote an English friend, observing that "Charles Town the principle one in this province is a polite agreeable place, the people live very Gentilie and very much in the English Taste." Near the end of the colonial period an English traveler noted that the city "is now supposed to contain 9 or 10,000 white inhabitants and about 30,000 black Negro slaves." Although noting a growing "zeal for liberty" among the inhabitants, this visitor noted that "most people that are born in Carolina can't help discovering in common conversation a great partiality towards England, calling it home tho' they have never been there."

Even after the Revolution the "Englishness" of Charleston was more evident than that of any other American city. At the end of the eighteenth century an English student at Charleston College wrote his parents that "the manners of the people here, are much more polished than the Virginians, and approximate that of my Countrymen." He further asserted that nowhere "were any Women fonder of dress than the Charleston ladies, the fashions are not out in London three months before they become the rage here." Crèvecoeur, who had seen a great deal of America by the time he visited Charleston in 1782, wrote that "an European at his first arrival must be greatly surprised when he sees the elegance of their houses, their sumptuous furniture, as well as the magnificence of their tables. Can he imagine himself in a country the establishment of which is so recent?" "Of all the towns in North America," as J. F. D. Smyth wrote at about the same time, Charleston was "the one in which the conveniences of luxury are most to be met with."

The per capita wealth of Charleston indeed was the greatest of all the American cities for much of the eighteenth century. Situated on a neck of land formed by the confluence of the Ashley and Cooper rivers—or, in the tongue-in-cheek description Charlestonians prefer, where the Ashley and Cooper join to form the Atlantic

Ocean—Charleston was one of America's busiest deepwater ports. Josiah Quincy wrote from the city in 1773 that "the number of shipping far surpassed all I had ever seen in Boston . . . about 350 sail lay off the town." Although the development of Charleston neck was not begun until seventy years after the first Virginia settlers dropped anchor off the site of Jamestown, the city and its commerce grew at an astounding rate. John Lawson reported in 1709 that South Carolina "is in as thriving circumstances at this time, as any colony on the continent of English America." The exportation of rice, naval stores, and later indigo provided ready wealth to Low Country planters.

The Charleston area was settled initially by Barbadians, some of whom later formed the core developers of the Cape Fear region of southeastern North Carolina. The continued influx of South Carolinians into the Cape Fear made it a cultural extension of the Low Country. The same was true of the Georgia coast, which was dominated by commerce from Charleston, and so even the city of Savannah is considered to be within the cultural boundary of the Low Country.

Although Charleston was known for its "English Taste," the city actually saw a very significant settlement of other ethnic groups, and indeed it had the most "foreign" aspect of any city in America. Foremost among these groups were French Huguenots, who even before the end of the seventeenth century rose to positions of wealth and political power in the colony. The architecture and arts, particularly the furniture, reveal the presence of French-trained tradesmen. Germans, too, represented a sizable component of Charleston's population. There is relatively little evidence of Germanic style in the arts of the city, but a smattering of objects with a Teutonic background remains from the Salzburger settlement near Savannah.

As in Britain and the Chesapeake, there was a certain preference for conservative furnishings in Charleston. In 1771 Peter Manigault sent his London factor a list of furniture and silver to be purchased, "the plainer the better so that they are fashionable." Other wealthy Charlestonians had more sumptuous tastes. In 1770 Jo-

Humphrey Sommers House exterior, Charleston, South Carolina, c. 1769.

siah Quincy: "Dined with considerable company at Miles Brewton Esqr's, a gentleman of very large fortune: a most superb house said to have cost him 8000£ sterling. The grandest hall I ever beheld, azure blue satin window curtains, rich blue paper with gilt, mashee borders, most elegant pictures, excessive grand and costly looking glasses etc." Brewton's "grandest hall" had painted blue paper in the ceiling vaults, edged with elaborate gilt papier-mâché borders, a room finish that had only just come into vogue in London by the time Brewton's house was finished in 1769.

A year later, Lieutenant William Bull wrote the Earl of Hillsborough in a lengthy report to the Board of Trade, assuring London that "our houses are plain but convenient," much in contrast to the "state, magnificence and ostentation, the natural attendants of riches"

that Quincy observed. Bull made further efforts to represent the colony as no threat to British economy, suggesting that "attempts to establish" manufactures in South Carolina "can never succeed to any degree, where there is so much room to employ labour in agriculture and trade with more profit." "Cards, dice, the bottle and horses," he observed, "engross prodiguous portions of time and attention," diversions also typical of English gentry of the period.

"The Rice swamps begin 10 or 12 Miles distance" from Charleston, as John Mair observed in 1791. Inland from the sea breezes that swept through Charleston, however, was an insufferable experience. "Every planter that can afford it," Mair noted, "has a residence" in the city, for as a Scots visitor wrote in 1810, "This climate is probably the most trying of any." The summer heat, even in

Sommers parlor, Charleston, South Carolina, c. 1769.

Charleston, contributed to an "atmosphere, in which One can hardly breath[e], which dispels sleap from the fatigued system & makes Life a Burthen." Not a few Charlestonians escaped the "noxious vapours" of the Low Country summer by fleeing to more pleasant climes; Newport, Rhode Island, was a favored escape well before the Revolution.

The situation was little better in other areas of the Low Country. A resident of Savannah wrote a friend in Boston to discourage New England artisans from making a move to Georgia, where of emigrant northerners "three fourths who spent their summers here, leave their bones." The "grave digger in Savannah," as this wag observed, "is the most independent planter in the state of Georgia." Visiting the northern Low Country in the 1770s, Scotswoman Janet Schaw wrote that the "peas-antry" of the Cape Fear spent much of their time "sitting under a rustick shade, drinking New England rum made into grog, the most shocking liquor you can imagine." This left these denizens of the pine barrens with "sallow complexions and languid eyes . . . their joints loose and their walk uneven."

Notwithstanding the rigors of the Low Country climate, which long has been esteemed a "heaven in the spring, hell in the summer, and a hospital in the fall," the arts flourished in Charleston through the Neoclassical period. As in the Chesapeake, the economy of the region began a significant shift. Rice and indigo gave way to King Cotton, particularly the sea island variety. Cotton brought new prosperity even to the already prosperous Cape Fear, which before the Revolution had been the principal colonial exporter of tar, pitch, turpentine,

Sommers bedroom, Charleston, South Carolina, c. 1769.

planking, and spars. With this development came a lessening of Charleston's economic dominance of the area; as the cotton agronomy developed in the Low Country, large plantations became major independent economic units, and city fortunes amassed from mercantilism and factorage declined. However, from the settlement of the Low Country until the Panic of 1819 and afterward, its wealthy inhabitants were able to patronize Charleston's fashionable artists and artisans as well as those from the northern centers of the arts, particularly New York, that burgeoned after the Revolution.

Very fine representations of Baroque, Rococo, and Neoclassical visual and decorative arts were produced in the area, especially Charleston. Most of the Low Country's artisans, like those of the Chesapeake, followed the English styles closely, although there were more

opulent and urban aspects to much of their work, even in the smaller towns of the region. Early-eighteenth-century Charleston furniture, for example, often accords closely with the architectural books of the period such as William Salmon's *Palladio Londinensis*, and the design of the furniture produced later in the century generally was drawn from the works of Chippendale and others. Charleston and other Low Country artists and artisans also kept abreast of changing Neoclassical styles and technology after the Revolution. It was the almost overwhelming demand for New York imports in the second and third decades of the nineteenth century that effectively slowed and eventually halted regional production in the Low Country.

Whitehall dining room, Berkeley County, South Carolina, 1818.

1 Gateleg table, Charleston, 1700–1710. Although Charleston developed a significant class of "mechanicks" in various trades during the seventeenth century, objects made in the city before 1720 are rare. This walnut table (see p. 16 for full view) has balustrade leg turnings of a form that is common on tables from the coastal cities and towns of Massachusetts and Connecticut, and the table very likely would have been attributed to New England were it not for the presence of a cypress drawer frame and a yellow pine drawer bottom. Cypress is considered a hallmark of Low Country furniture; although it is native to the coastal areas from Maryland south to Florida, the wood is rarely encountered in furniture made north of the Lower Chesapeake region, and it was the predominant conifer used by Charleston cabinetmakers. This table descended in the Laurens family, probably from the parents of the prominent merchant and patriot Henry Laurens (1724–92). *Acc. 2037-2.*   JB

2 Couch, Charleston, 1720–30. Often known as a "day bed" today, in the seventeenth and early eighteenth centuries such a piece generally was listed in inventories as a "couch." The earliest known mention of the form in Charleston is a description of a piece in the effects of Colonel William Rhett in 1719 as "one cain couch." The MESDA example was fitted with a woven cane bottom in the nineteenth century, but originally was finished with a "sacking" or canvas bottom tacked into a rabbet in the frame. Sacking usually consisted of a wide hemmed skirt with sewn grommets to receive a rope lacing that filled the void between. This permitted the sacking to be tightened periodically. A "squab" or cushion usually covered the couch. John Boyden's Charleston inventory of 1726 listed a "couch and squabb," and the fact that these pieces were used for sleeping is suggested by the description of a "couch bed stead" found in several Low Country inventories.

This couch, almost eighty-one inches long and quite wide, is larger than most examples from Britain and the northern colonies. The organic nature of the crest carving (the top of the crest is missing), the sinuous back stiles, and the inverted "cup" form of the splat suggest a Continental origin for the maker, possibly German or French. The stiles are a flattened version of twisted columns carved with running leafy vines—a favored motif in German Baroque churches. *Acc. 3490.*   JB

3 Chalice, by Miles Brewton, Charleston, 1711. The earliest dated example of southern silver, this chalice is engraved in Roman letters "Belonging to St. Thomas Parish in South Carolina Anno Dom: 1711." Bearing the mark "MB" in a shield, the chalice was made by Miles Brewton, who arrived in South Carolina in 1684. After that date, Brewton was not mentioned in Charleston records again until 1702, when he assisted in the appraisal of the estate of William Slow. Another appraiser of the estate was Nicholas DeLonguemare, a silversmith, which suggests a possible trade connection between the two artisans. Other silversmiths in Charleston at the time were Solomon Legare (1674–1760) and Peter Jacob Guerard; the latter arrived in Charleston in 1680. Three additional ecclesiastical pieces by Brewton exist: two chalices and a paten. Brewton served in various civic offices, but his 1743 will described him simply as "Miles Brewton of Charlestown . . . Gold Smith." His son Robert followed him in the trade. His grandson Miles Brewton garnered one of the most considerable fortunes in the colony and during 1765–69 built America's finest existing colonial townhouse at 27 King Street.

On loan to the museum, acc. 3452. JB

4 Joined stand, Charleston, 1720–30. This stand has a long history of ownership in the Miles Brewton house in Charleston, but its origin and early history are unknown. Made entirely of cypress, the piece bears a similarity to the common British and New England joined, or "joint," stool, but the overhang of the top on this example makes it impractical for sitting. Two pieces of the top had broken away for that reason. A more logical explanation is documented in Plate 6 of William Hogarth's famed series of engravings entitled *A Harlot's Progress*, published in London in 1732. The scene shows a coffin resting on two oval-topped stands with vasiform legs and a third stand nearby. These were "bier" stands, made in pairs and specifically intended for the "laying out" of the deceased before interment. The elongated balusters of the legs and delicate stretchers of this stand, which does not appear to have been painted, suggest a date later than other early joined stools.

Gift of Mr. and Mrs. Ralph P. Hanes, acc. 2414-2. JB

5 *Mrs. Samuel Prioleau*, pastel on paper, by Henrietta Johnston, Charleston, 1715. Henrietta Johnston was the first known pastellist to work in the American colonies, as well as the first professional female portraitist. Married to Gideon Johnston, Commissary for the Bishop of London in Charles Town, she left Ireland for South Carolina with her husband in 1708. Plagued by debts, the Johnstons eked out a meager living in the colony with the help of Henrietta's earnings as a portraitist. Johnston wrote the Bishop in 1709: "Were it not for the assistance my wife gives me by drawing Pictures (which can last but a little time in a place so ill peopled) I should not have been able to live." Johnston died in 1716, and Henrietta for the most part maintained her residence in Charles Town and continued drawing. She died in March 1729 and was buried in St. Philip's churchyard.

Henrietta's work has been compared to that of Simon Digby and Edward Luttrell, both Irishmen, and she may have been a pupil of either or both. Her style is easily recognizable: heads quarter turned, generally dark and well-defined eyes, and softly draped gowns on female subjects. The hair of her ladies falls over one shoulder; her men wear wigs with cascading curls. Her only known attempts at landscape backgrounds appear in her drawings of children.

Mrs. Samuel Prioleau, née Mary Magdalen Gendron, was the wife of Colonel Samuel Prioleau, a Charleston silversmith. Her pastel portrait was signed by the artist and is one of four by Henrietta Johnston on exhibit at MESDA, including one of Colonel Prioleau. *Acc. 2048-2.* FA

6 Earthenware jar, attributed to Andrew Duche, New Windsor or Savannah, Georgia, 1735–48. Andrew Duche was the son of the Philadelphia potter Anthony Duche, Sr., who was active from 1724 to 1762. After working in his father's factory, Andrew moved to Charleston in the early 1730s and then to New Windsor, Georgia. By 1736 he had relocated to Savannah, where he worked until the mid-1740s. During this period, Duche claimed that he had "found out the true manner of making porcelain or china ware," and repeatedly sought funding from England to finance his ventures.

A long Georgia history and the similarity of the "A" in its "AD" mark to that of the "AD" found on stoneware shards excavated at Anthony Duche's Philadelphia site account for this lead-glazed redware jar's attribution. *Acc. 3440.* FA

7 Table, northeastern coast of Georgia, 1735–40. Although there was a consistent influx of Germans into Charleston during the colonial period, the most cohesive German settlement in the Low Country was near the city of Savannah. In 1734 the Reverend Johann Martin Bolzius (1703–65) accompanied nearly fifty German and Austrian Lutherans fleeing the oppression of the Archbishopric of Salzburg, centered in the city of that name in the Austrian Alps near the Bavarian border. Three additional groups of the Salzburgers, as they were called, followed, and German Protestants from Wurttemberg joined the settlement during the 1750s.

The earliest known example of Georgia furniture, with legs of sweet gum, a poplar frame, and yellow pine stretchers, this table obviously is a product of the Salzburger settlement. Its stylistic heritage, including the deep frame, splayed legs, and flat stretchers, is clearly derived from south German and northern Austrian prototypes. The dovetailed frame conceals a storage area that can be reached only by removing the replaced top, and the top is attached to the sides with pins that pierce dovetailed battens, a standard Germanic construction method. *Acc. 2082.* JB

8 Dressing table, Charleston, 1735–50. This dressing table is of walnut with cypress and yellow pine secondary woods. The use of walnut on such a relatively early piece is not unusual in the Low Country, for it was not until the middle of the eighteenth century that shipments to Charleston of mahogany from Campeche and the British West Indies increased and walnut furniture became rare. The table suggests a blending of both Continental and British stylistic influence. The sides of the top are separate pieces mitered to the principal top boards, a Baroque detail; the fleur-de-lis-like carving on the knees could be taken as French. The most unusual decorative detail is the shells, which spring from the knees up to the leg stiles, a carving feature more often associated with chairs than tables. The rounded leg stiles also are a chairmaker's convention. These details cannot be related easily to other Charleston work. However, the general stance of the table is British, and graceful pad feet with well-defined turned nosing over cylindrical "discs" and a gentle curve where they meet the leg are characteristic of Charleston. The same is true of the drawer construction. The drawer bottoms are fitted into rabbets, and run on full-length strips glued next to the drawer sides. The 1733 inventory of Jonathan Main of Charleston lists two dressing tables, one "with three drawers" for £5. This example descended in the Smyth family of Charleston. *Acc. 2024-33.* *JB*

9 Easy chair, Charleston, 1735–45. All southern easy chairs are rare, but those made during the colonial period are exceptionally so. One of the earliest surviving examples from the South, and certainly the earliest piece of seating furniture from the Low Country, is this easy chair of mahogany, which has mahogany, ash, cypress, and poplar secondary woods. The most uniquely Charleston feature of this chair is the massive, blocklike rear feet. The front face of the back legs is straight, yet the back of the leg forms a graceful curve. The commodious width of the chair is also typical of the Low Country. A 1742 Charleston inventory listed an "Easie Chair & Cushion, covered with Crewell Wrought and an old Calicoe Cushion Case £30." Such chairs often were intended for bedchamber use, and indeed not a few of them were made like a chair described in the 1742 inventory of the Reverend James Parker as "a Close Stool Easy Chair." Many of them were listed with slip cases that protected expensive primary coverings such as the replica green worsted moreen with a vermiculated pattern on the MESDA example. Nail evidence on the chair frame reveals that no upholstery nails ornamented the surface originally.

The chair descended in the Cannon and Fraser families of Charleston. Daniel Cannon (1726–1802) was a prominent building contractor in the city; he married Martha Winn in 1750. It is possible that Cannon inherited the chair from his father, who died in 1743 after a residence of only three years in the city. *Acc. 2788-2.* *JB*

10   *Mrs. Algernon Wilson*, oil on canvas, by Jeremiah Theus, Charleston, 1756. Jeremiah Theus was colonial South Carolina's most popular painter; over 170 works have been attributed to him. Born in Switzerland, Theus emigrated with his family to South Carolina about 1735, first to Orangeburgh Township and then to Charleston, where he was advertising as early as 1740. He married twice and died in 1774. Like many of his colonial colleagues, Theus based the clothing and poses of many of his sitters on English engravings, but the formality and rigidity of his subjects and their costume were derived from the German Baroque. The flowing flowers in this portrait are an Italian Baroque motif not usually used by Theus.

Sarah Proctor Daniel married Algernon Wilson, a wealthy planter, in 1746. She was descended from Landgrave Robert Daniel, Deputy Governor of South Carolina during 1716–17. *Acc. 2024-52.*   *FA*

1.OK OUKAH ULAH. 2.K.SKALILOSKEN KETAGUSTAH 3.T TATHTOWE. [4 C CLOGOITTAH. [5. K KOLLANNAH.[6. U UKWANEEQUA.[7. O ONACONOA.]

The above Indian Kings or Chiefs Were brought over from Carolina, by Sʳ Alexander Coming Barᵗ (being the Chiefs of the Cherrokee Indians) to enter into Articles of Friendship and Commerce with his Majesty, th swere as they arriv'd they were conducted to Windsor, & were present at the Installation of Prince William & the Lᵈ Chesterfield. The Pomp & Splendour of the Court, and ⸿ Grandeur, not only of the Ceremony as well of the Place, now what Struck them with infinite Surprize and Wonder. They were handsomely entertain'd at his Majesty's Charge, & Cloath'd with These Habits out of ⸿ Royal Wardrobe. When the Court left Windsor they were brought to ⸿ Town and proper Lodgings & Attendance provided for them near Covent Garden. They were entertain'd at all ⸿ Publick Diversions of the Town, and carried to all Places of Note & Curiosity. They were remarkably Strict in their Probits and Monday Their Beha- vieur very courteous, and their Gratitude to his Majesty was often expressed in a publick Manner for ⸿ many Favours they receiv'd. — On Monday Sepᵗ 7, 1730, Articles of Friendship and Commerce were accordingly proposed to them by 2 Commissioners to ⸿ Lords and Plantations who were agreed on Two Days after, viz on ⸿ 9ᵗʰ at Whitehall, and Sign'd on ⸿ Part of their Lordships by Alured Popple Esqʳ upon wᶜʰ KETAGUSTAH after a Short Speech, in Complement to his Majesty Concluded A by laying down his Feathers upon ⸿ Table & said, This is our Way of Talking, wᶜʰ is ⸿ Same Thing to us, as ⸿ Letters in ⸿ Books are to you; and to you BELOVED MEN, we deliver these Feathers in Confirmation of all that we have said. — Nᴮ The marks on their Faces & Bodys are tokens of Victory.

II *Cherokee Indians*, engraved by J. Basire, London, 1740–50. The legend at the bottom of this copper-plate line engraving marked "engraved by J. Basire after MARKHAM" identifies the Indians as (from left to right, with more proper spellings) Oukoun-aco, Kitagista, Kilonah, Oukah-Ulah, Tiftowe, Clogoitah, and Onokanowin. These were the seven chiefs of the Cherokee Nation, which occupied parts of present-day North and South Carolina and Tennessee. In 1730 Sir Alexander Coming took them to England, where they made an agreement with King George II to trade only with the English, to allow no other white men to settle in their country, to aid the English in war, and to permit white offenders in their nation to be punished by English law.

American Indians were popular subjects for English portraitists and engravers in the early and mid-eighteenth century. A series of engravings of Indian kings dating about 1710 is in the Winterthur collection. *Acc. 2472.*   FA

12

Dressing table, Charleston, 1740–45. The taste for "neat and plain" even in wealthy Chesapeake households had its counterpart in the Low Country, and the conservative transitional style and very British aspect of this mahogany table reflect that taste. The Baroque shaping of the skirt, rather abrupt knees, and greater "lift" of the curve of the pad feet relate this example to a number of other tables from the same shop. The table was never fitted with drops, despite the shaping of the skirt. Two of the chased brasses are original and help in assigning a probable date range for the table. Such brasses were rapidly declining in favor by the early 1740s; these are transitional in nature, since they employ cast posts rather than wire or "cotter pin" fasteners. *Acc. 950-7.* JB

13

Pier table, Charleston, 1740–50. The low height of this table, twenty-seven inches, and its substantial width, forty-two inches, may qualify it as an exceptionally rare survival of a side table intended for use under a large pier glass, but its actual intended use is unknown. The flattened, peaked arches of the skirt as well as the ovolo top molding with indented corners relate the table to the previous dressing table, and construction details shared by both include mahogany rear rails and the extensive evidence of tooth-planing on interior surfaces. Drawer construction and a different leg and foot formula, however, indicate a different shop. The drawer of this example, although molded, does not lip over the frame, an early detail. The brasses are original and marked "I. BATES" on the rear, presumably the name of a Birmingham brassfounder. *Acc. 2764.* JB

14

Card table, Charleston, 1745–55. The 1739 inventory of Maurice Lewis of Charleston lists a "mahogany card table" valued at £6, very likely a conservative example like this one. The taste for such unadorned pieces continued to the end of the colonial period; in 1768 Thomas Elfe made Elizabeth Pinckney "2 plain mahogany card tables" for £40. The projecting front corners of this table are common to Charleston gaming tables of the period, as is the drawer fitted to the front of the frame. The cock-beading of the drawer indicates a slightly later date than the preceding tables. That this piece has pad feet is not a sure indication of an early date, for such feet were utilized almost to the end of the Rococo period in Charleston. This example has a plain top, but broadcloth-covered tables certainly were familiar in the city. Elfe's account book contains a 1772 entry for "lining a card table £3."

Gift of Mr. and Mrs. Frank A. Liggett, acc. 3266.

JB

15

Slab table, Charleston, 1745–55. Sideboard tables were in use from the seventeenth century. Many of them were fitted with marble slabs, and in Charleston they frequently were listed in inventories as a "marble slab and frame." In 1734 Samuel Jennings advertised "Eight very fine & curious Indian Marble Tables . . . all ready moulded and finely polished." The "curious" meant "elegant" in the vernacular of the time; these tables probably were English, with frames of walnut or mahogany, and fitted with marble cut in India. A 1750 inventory listing that might well have described MESDA's table was that of Robert Thorpe: "one marble slab with mahogany frame £20."

The MESDA table is notable for its coved frame in the Chinese taste; its facings conceal the upper leg stiles, a sophisticated urban detail. The claw feet, familiarly known in Charleston as "eagle's claws" during the colonial period, have well-rounded balls and strongly projecting talons, a typical regional form. The table is made of dark and dense mahogany generally taken to be from Santo Domingo; this is typical of most Charleston tables of this period. The same form of sideboard table frequently was made with a wooden top, and an all-mahogany table from the same shop as the MESDA example has been recorded.

An interesting event in 1792 involved a sideboard table. A Charleston householder had "accidently placed" a "globular decanter" on the interior sill of "a window fronting the south." The house "narrowly escaped being consumed," for "The rays of the sun passing through the decanter, collected to a focus, and set fire to a mahogany slab, which instantly kindled into a blaze."

Mr. and Mrs. Gordon Hanes, Mr. and Mrs. Leland Short, and Mr. and Mrs. James R. Melchor Purchase Funds, acc. 3163.

JB

16 Chest of drawers, Charleston, 1730–40. The early use of mahogany in Charleston, as well as the Low Country's eager acceptance of urban British style, is evident in this small chest of drawers. The top and drawer fronts are of what generally was known in the eighteenth century as "island" mahogany, now often known as "Cuban" although the material came from a number of the Caribbean islands. The "island" wood is characterized by strong mineral streaking, whereas the "bay" mahogany described in early accounts often was plain and unfigured. The bay in question was the Bay of Campeche, where Honduras mahogany was the primary export staple; the sides of this chest are made from that wood. This chest of drawers, the earliest known Charleston case piece, descended in the family of Daniel Cannon, who owned the easy chair illustrated earlier (9). The brasses are replacements based on the evidence of wire attachments for the bails. The hardware evidence, along with the presence of molded, unlipped drawers, verifies an early date for the piece. Typical of Charleston chests of drawers is the lack of a rail above the upper drawer. The top is fitted to the sides of the carcass with a single dovetail run the full depth of the sides, a construction detail also found in Massachusetts and Virginia.

Gift of Mr. and Mrs. E. Norwood Robinson, acc. 2785.

JB

17

Cabinet on chest, Charleston, 1740–50. At the time this mahogany and cypress cabinet on chest was made, the only design sources available to cabinet-makers were architectural books and drawings. Eighteenth-century designers such as William Kent, William Salmon, and Batty Langley drew on the works of Andrea Palladio (1508–80) and Inigo Jones (1573–1652), publishing architectural design books that were used by Low Country artisans as well as their English and northern counterparts. The classical interior and exterior elevations of the Low Country's Drayton Hall and Pompion Hill Chapel were derived from such design sources. Indeed, elements of the scrolled pediment and pineapple finial of this cabinet on chest can be found on a doorway of the composite order found in William Salmon's *Palladio Londinensis*, published in 1734. Details in the cabinet section of the chest, including the pineapple finial, can be seen in Batty Langley's *City and Country Builder's and Workman's Treasury of Designs* of 1740, which also contains twenty-five furniture designs popularized by Kent.

The history of the chest can be traced to William Loughton Smith (1758–1812), whose father was the prominent Charleston merchant Benjamin Smith. Benjamin Smith married Ann Loughton (d. 1760) and Mary Wragg, and the chest may originally have been owned by one of them.

Donated by Mr. and Mrs. George Kaufman in memory of Polly and Frank Myers, acc. 3522.   FA

18 Pair of sauceboats, by Daniel You, Charleston, 1750. The engraved initials on these pieces verify that they were owned by Daniel and Martha Cannon. Their marriage in 1750 almost certainly dates the manufacture of these sauceboats, for silversmith Daniel You died the same year. You was working in the city as early as 1737, and is thought to have been the father of Thomas You, another prominent Charleston silversmith. The wide, squat form of these boats and the robust design of the cast handles and feet are early details. In the MESDA collection are a pair of tablespoons by the same maker, bearing the same "D. YOU" mark as the sauceboats. A large group of silver marked "ĐY" and showing French influence has been attributed to You, but it is post-Revolutionary and represents the work of another silversmith. *Acc. 3407-1 & 2.*

JB

19 Covered sugar bowl, by Thomas You, Charleston, 1753–65. One of only two known pieces of Rococo chased silver made in Charleston, this sugar bowl, like the preceding sauceboats, bears the initials of Daniel and Mary Cannon. Eighteenth-century southern hollow ware is rare; this piece is one of four known examples of raised work by You. The other three pieces are a footed bowl, a pap boat, and a "cann," or tulip-shaped mug. Covered sugar bowls such as this one were identified by a different term in some inventories. In her will of 1717, Elizabeth Bridger of Isle of Wight County, Virginia, left her granddaughter "the Silver Sugar box." The use of "box" has not been noted in Low Country records.

The relatively low chasing of the You bowl and the apparent lack of detail on the decoration make the work seem simple in execution, but extensive polishing over time has obliterated some of the line-engraved detail on the surface. The pineapple finial is composed of a pair of castings. Thomas You advertised frequently "at the Sign of the Golden Cup" in Queen Street, particularly during the 1760s and early 1770s. He also did at least some copperplate engraving, advertising in 1765 that he had finished engraving the "West Prospect of St. Philip's Church." The sugar bowl is marked "T.Y" three times on the bottom. Multiple strikes of a maker's mark were common on Charleston silver. *Acc. 2506.*

JB

20 Desk and bookcase, Charleston, 1765–80. This mahogany and cypress desk and bookcase, with a broken pediment and a plinth supporting a separate scrolled shell, reflects the popularity of architectural design in the South Carolina Low Country in the mid-eighteenth century. Denticulation on the pediment and bookcase crown moldings, a front frieze pattern of diamonds interlaced with ovals, fluted and stop-fluted pilasters with bases and capitols, and egg-and-dart carving on the rails and stiles surrounding the mirrored doors are all architectural elements characteristic of Charleston work of the period. The fret and carved edge at the mirrors are features that also can be found in the woodwork of Pompion Hill Chapel and St. James Church, both located near Charleston.

Charleston cabinetmakers were advertising desks and bookcases as early as January 1733. On 22 March 1740, Josiah Claypoole, a Charleston cabinetmaker originally from Philadelphia, advertised in the *South Carolina Gazette* that he had "Desk and Book Cases, with Arch'd Pediment and OG Heads, Common Desks of all Sorts" for sale. Thomas Elfe recorded a number of desks and bookcases in his account book, one of the more elaborate being "a mahogany desk and bookcase Chineas dores" that he sold for £130. *Acc. 845.* *FA*

21 Detail of *A Map of South Carolina and Part of Georgia*, engraved by Thomas Jefferys, London, 1757. This detail, taken from the lower righthand corner of a map engraved from surveys made by William Bull, Captain Gascoign, Hugh Bryan, and William DeBrahm, depicts slaves involved in the production of dye from indigo, one of the Low Country's main cash crops during the mid-eighteenth century. Several steps were necessary for extracting the dye from indigo plants. In South Carolina, the plants were gathered and fermented in large vats of water. After fermentation, the water was drained off into another vat located below the first and beaten gently with wooden paddles to eliminate gas. When that operation was completed, a valve at the bottom of the vat was opened and the liquid ran out, leaving a residue that was put into linen bags and hung to dry. The dye was then spread into boxes three feet long and two feet wide, cut into two-inch square cubes, and packed for shipping. The man in the foreground of this detail is cutting the indigo into cubes; those in the background appear to be taking down the drying linen bags. *Acc. 3024-2.* *FA*

22 *Mrs. John Beale*, oil on canvas, by John Wollaston, Charleston, 1765–67. John Wollaston was one of the most influential painters in the colonies during the eighteenth century. He and Joseph Blackburn, another Englishman, are credited with the introduction to the colonies of the English Rococo approach to portraiture. His characteristic almond-shaped eyes, fabric treatment, and poses are all reflected in the works of John Hesselius and Henry Benbridge and the early paintings of John Singleton Copley and Benjamin West.

Wollaston, the son of John Woolaston [*sic*], a London portraitist and violinist, is known to have painted at least 300 portraits. He was probably trained in portraiture by his father and Thomas Hudson, a popular London artist, and it is thought that in London he specialized in the painting of clothing. From 1749 to 1758, Wollaston worked in New York, Maryland, Virginia, and Philadelphia. After leaving the colonies briefly, he worked in Charleston from 1765 to 1767. He was recorded in Southampton, England, in 1775, but nothing further is known about his life.

Mrs. John Beale, née Mary Ross, was married on 18 March 1762 in St. Andrew's Parish. Her husband was a merchant and the son of Othniel Beale. She died on 29 November 1771 after giving birth to a daughter, Mary Hannah. This portrait was identified by a miniature of the painting in the MESDA collection inscribed "Mary/ Mrs. Beale/ nee Ross/ M. Aged 25." The turning of the lace at the lower left of the portrait is a technique that also was used in Hudson's studio and suggests Wollaston's training there as a drapery artist. The frame is contemporary to the painting but not original.

Gift of Mrs. Jan Mendall Lewis, acc. 3050.   *FA*

23

A View of Charles Town, oil on canvas, by Thomas Leech (Leitch), 1774. According to the *South Carolina Gazette* of 25 October 1773, Thomas Leech arrived in Charleston from London that year. His seascape of Charleston was first advertised in the spring of 1774, and again on 17 October of that year in the *South Carolina Gazette*: "PROPOSALS for publishing by SUBSCRIPTION, a View of Charles TOWN: THIS View has been taken with the greatest Accuracy and Care by Mr. Leech, who is now employed about painting a finished Picture from the Drawings already made by him . . . and will be so exact a Portrait of the Town . . . that every House in View will be distinctly known . . . the two greatest Artists in the World, Messrs. *Woollett*

and *Smith* have been engaged to engrave it." One of these prints is in the MESDA collection (24).

This view of Charleston was painted in the "Dutch manner," a style popular in the seventeenth century in the Netherlands and later in England, depicting the sea, ships, and figures working aboard the vessels. Characteristic of this type of seascape are the strong vertical line of the sailing ship and the expanse of water represented in this particular example. Much of this seascape is identifiable: the land in the foreground is Shute's Folly, the church in the center is St. Michael's, the building to the right of the church is the Exchange, and the house with columns on the extreme right is the Charles Pinckney house, built in the 1740s. *Acc. 2024-30.*

FA

A View of CHARLES-TOWN, the Capital of SOUTH CAROLINA.

24

A View of Charles-Town, the Capital of South Carolina, from an Original Picture Painted at Charlestown in the Year 1774, engraved by Samuel Smith, London, 1776. Engraved from the Thomas Leech painting of Charleston (23), this print was published on 3 June 1776 in London. In 1774, advertisements in the *South Carolina Gazette* offered subscriptions for 300 prints "at so low a Price as a Guinea a Piece." The notice also promised that the print would "be ready to be delivered by the *First* of *January,* 1776."
Acc. 2024-29. FA

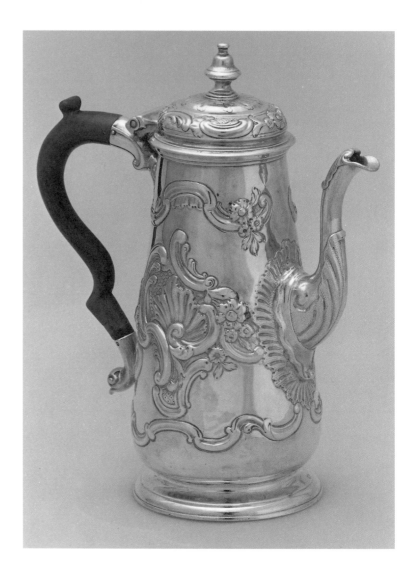

26 Salver, by Alexander Petrie, Charleston, 1750–60. Variously described as salvers, waiters, and even trays, depending on their size, these objects were used for a number of purposes, including the service of tea and coffee. It has been suggested that small salvers such as this example were often used in conjunction with a teapot or coffeepot alone. Petrie's own inventory indicates as much, for it lists "1 Large Chased Coffee pott and Stand 46½ Oz. @ 40/ [£]93." Petrie also owned a "Large Waiter" weighing 22½ ounces. The rims of small salvers were often cast in a single piece, as this example was, with the sheet-silver bottom and the cast feet applied below with silver solder. The rims of large salvers, or waiters, normally were cast in sections. This salver, which provided the design for MESDA's logo, descended in the Peronneau and Finley families. It was purchased at the estate sale of Henry Bailey of Edisto Island, who had directed in his 1764 will that all his personal effects "be sold at publick Vendue." *Acc. 2024-48.* *JB*

25 Coffeepot, by Alexander Petrie, Charleston, 1750–60. One of the finest known examples of southern Rococo silver, this coffeepot is one of only a handful of examples of southern chased work. Other surviving repoussé pieces, with the exception of the Thomas You sugar bowl (19), are by Baltimore and Annapolis makers. Three other coffeepots by Petrie are known, one of them in the MESDA collection with a history of descent in the Ravenel family. Although the other pots are plain-bodied, they all share the castings used on the chased pot, including the hinge, handle sockets, spout, and foot ring. Each of the pots is of seamed construction, with a vertical joint located under the handle sockets; this was not unusual on essentially straight-bodied pots in the George II style.

Little is known of Alexander Petrie's background, but it is likely that he was trained in Britain. First listed in Charleston records in 1744, he died in 1768, esteemed a man of "Fair Character" who had "acquired a handsome Fortune" and "had some Time ago retired from Business." Nevertheless, at the time of his death he owned a full complement of silversmith's tools as well as a valuable slave, Abraham, who was a silversmith. Petrie's fortune was derived from land speculation and an extensive lending operation, not unusual for a colonial silversmith. He held over £11,000 in notes and bonds at his death. This pot, marked "AP" four times on the bottom, was found by a Canadian collector in England, where it might have been taken by a fleeing loyalist, a member of the British occupying forces during the 1782 evacuation of Charleston, or a member of the Laurens family, to whom Petrie was related by marriage. Petrie's estate inventory lists nearly one hundred pieces of household silver, including two silver-mounted fowling pieces, a silver-hilted sword, and "1 New Chased Coffee pott 32½ Ozs. @ 50/. . . . . . [£]81..5..0." The MESDA pot bears the scratched weight "31½" on the bottom. *Acc. 3996.* *JB*

27 Easy chair, Charleston, 1760–75. Existing Charleston easy chairs of this period have the same basic frame form, including crest and side shaping and the form of the arm cones; the construction of these chairs is exceptionally consistent. This example (see p. 70 for full view) varies from two other MESDA examples only in its employment of a "commode," or rounded, front rail and curved side rails. Secondary woods include mahogany, poplar, yellow pine, and red bay. Bay is a swamp wood that is seldom encountered in furniture, although it is mentioned in records. Somewhat similar to Honduras mahogany in grain structure, it actually belongs to the laurel family. This chair's "eagle's claw" feet, as Elfe and others called them, are closely related to those on a MESDA bedstead. The knee carving shows the same hand as a bedstead in the collection of the Charleston Museum. This carver's style included the highly repetitive use of chip-cuts made with a gouge. A particularly strong Charleston detail is the unusual "gunstock" profile of the rear legs, almost a reverse of the cabriole shape of the front legs. The chair descended from Dr. Richard Baker of Archdale Hall on the Ashley River. *Acc. 1045.* *JB*

28 Double chest with secretary, Charleston, 1755–75. The popular term "chest-on-chest" was not one used in early Low Country inventories. Instead, "double chest of drawers" was the accepted description of a large case piece such as this one (right), occurring as early as 1734.

This example is a showcase of classic Charleston details. The cornice is made up of an ogee crown, a Doric dentil, and a cove, a format repeated on a number of related case pieces. The strongly architectural nature of this chest is typical of Charleston, including the engaged, stop-fluted pilasters, the cove-and-ovolo bed molding, and the inset base. Its drawer construction also is normal to the Low Country and follows London practice in the use of full-bottom dustboards and two-part drawer bottoms divided from front to rear by muntins, a feature that lessened possible damage from radically shifting humidity levels.

The fret pattern in the frieze below the cornice is one popularly known as the "Elfe" fret, after the cabinetmaker Thomas Elfe, to whom many pieces of furniture with this decoration have been attributed without documentation of any sort, though a very similar fret pattern was used in the Elfe shop. In December 1772 Elfe billed contractor John Fullerton £1:10 for "a frett," and a month later charged the same builder for a total of 100 feet and "2 ps" of fret. At about the same time, Fullerton was building a frame house on Legare Street that still exists; in it is a figure-eight fret that differs only slightly from that on MESDA's double chest. An overmantel in the Heyward House on Church Street has a fret identical to the chest's; the same pattern has been seen on British furniture, but no published design source for it is known.

Double chests fitted with desk drawers evidently were made in Britain from the first quarter of the eighteenth century. They were expensive; in 1772 Elfe charged Mary Broughton £95 for a "doble chest drawers with a Desk Drawer," and the following year he charged Humphrey Sommers £80 for a "double chest of drawers with a frett round," obviously without a desk drawer.

Gift of Mr. and Mrs. Ralph P. Hanes, acc. 946. *JB*

29

Tea table, Charleston, 1765–75. Surprisingly, relatively little Charleston Rococo furniture carving matches the quality of the city's architectural carving during the period. However, there are a few pieces of Charleston furniture that can be linked to architectural work, and this tea table is one of them. The carver who executed much of the magnificent second-floor parlor entablature of the Brewton House also carved MESDA's table(see preface for detail of table carving), but the work cannot be attributed to Ezra Waite, the principal Brewton House carver. Like most Charleston tea tables, this one does not have a turning, or "birdcage," top. The gadrooning of the edge of the top is an unusual detail, but the elongated form of the pedestal vase is typical. This table descended in the Gibbes and Holmes families of Charleston. *Acc. 2181.* *JB*

30

Bedstead, Charleston, 1760–70. In 1772 Thomas Elfe billed Stephen Bull £50 for a "mahogany bedstead eagle claws & castors." Such a bedstead often cost less than the full hangings it required, owing to the enormous expense of fine fabrics. The partial hangings on the MESDA bed are a reproduction of a copperplate design used by the English fabric printer Robert Jones at his Old Ford works. The inventory of Thomas Middleton of Charleston listed "1 Suit Bed Furniture Jone's Pattern."

Elfe and other cabinetmakers frequently were employed to install and remove bed hangings according to seasonal changes. Summertime called for the removal of curtains and their replacement with "pavilions" of gauze to ward off mosquitos. Abiel Abbott wrote from Charleston in 1782 that those pests had "been prowling & singing every night & we have not quiet slumbers, except as we shrink behind our gauze rampart."

MESDA's bedstead, like most Charleston examples, has a headboard set between two pairs of mahogany strips attached to the headposts. This construction renders the headboard "removable," but no evidence supports the popular notion that such headboards actually were removed in hot weather. The same construction has been observed on bedsteads made in New York City. The feet of the headposts are a balustrade form evidently taken from Plate 32 of the second edition of Chippendale's *Director*. The cornice on this bed is a replica. Most formal beds were fitted with them, many replete with pulleys and other fittings for deploying the drapery.

Gift of Mr. and Mrs. Alban K. Barrus, acc. 3065.

JB

31 Side chair, Charleston, 1750–60. The notice of an estate sale at "Public Vendue" was posted in a 1779 Charleston newspaper, detailing "A Variety of Genteel household Furniture, amongst which are, twelve Cabriole Chairs." Ruth Bedon's estate inventory of 1765 lists "1 Doz. Mahogany Chairs with Eagles Claws £60." Despite such evidence, the MESDA side chair is one of only two known Charleston-made Rococo side chairs with cabriole legs and claw feet. The lack of such chairs, and the profusion of chairs in the Chinese taste—that is, with straight, or Marlborough, legs—very likely indicates that Charlestonians had embraced the more linear style at much the same time as it became fashionable in London during the 1740s. The splat of this chair is a modification of a design familiar all along the east coast. The chair descended in the Blake family of Charleston, probably from Edward Blake (d. 1795), a prominent merchant. The seat is covered with reproduction haircloth. George Parker of Charleston advertised in 1765 that he had imported "on the last Vessels from LONDON and BRISTOL . . . several neat horse hair Patterns for Chair Bottoms."

Gift of Mrs. J. William Haynie, acc. 3513.   *JB*

32 Bureau table, Charleston, 1750–65. Chippendale's *Director* illustrates "Buroe Tables," and a Charleston inventory of 1752 lists "A Mahogany Beaureau Table £9," its low valuation indicating that it very likely was old. May Lloyd's estate inventory of 1764, in contrast, contained "1 Beaurreau dressing Table" valued at £100; at that valuation the piece probably contained a fully fitted upper drawer, apparently a common feature of pieces intended for some other use than as a chest of drawers. Writing table versions, in fact, often had drawer fitments suited to that use. Interestingly, a 1797 Charleston advertisement offered sundry pieces of mahogany furniture, partly consisting of "Knee Chests of Drawers," a precursor of the modern term. This table is one of four Charleston examples known. The sides of the carcass are dovetailed to the top in the usual fashion. It is related to MESDA's double chest (28) in regard to the pattern of its feet and bed molding, but in this instance the cockbeading is applied to the case rather than to the drawers. The cabinet door conceals a single shelf; the brasses are original. *Acc. 3680.*   *JB*

33 Armchair, Charleston, 1765–75. Often listed in inventories as "elbow chairs" or "French chairs," chairs like this one were apparently produced in substantial numbers in Charleston. They are otherwise rare among forms of American seating furniture before the Neoclassical period, no doubt owing largely to the expense of the fully upholstered back. It is not known how early these chairs were described as "French," but clearly they were an English derivation of the *fauteuil* developed in Paris in the seventeenth century. British examples fully in the French manner were made, and were illustrated in the *Director*, but the Chinese detail and "tight," or squared-edge, upholstery favored by the British were not to be found on French armchairs during the Rococo period.

From the extensive study of inventories, it is apparent that "French" chairs in Charleston were ordered in pairs or sets. Elfe charged William Skirving £60 for "two French elbow chairs with hair seating" in 1771. A 1779 article in a Charleston paper described "twelve handsome French chairs" at the residence of Mrs. Rowan. Like the easy chairs, Charleston armchairs have generously wide proportions, usually more so than other American examples. This chair, which is virtually indistinguishable from English examples except for its secondary woods, here poplar, ash, cypress, and yellow pine, is upholstered in an antique French silk damask of the Louis XV period. It descended in the Rutledge family of Hampton Plantation. *Acc. 950-13.*

JB

34 Library bookcase, Charleston, 1765–75. This mahogany and cypress library bookcase (right) is very similar to that depicted in all three editions of Chippendale's *Director* (35). The design proportions were altered slightly to accommodate the tall ceilings in Charleston dwellings, and the four oval panels at the base were placed vertically. The fret design below the pediment is identical to that of the double chest of drawers illustrated earlier (28), suggesting a connection between the two pieces.

Bookcases were being sold in Charleston as early as the 1730s. Charles Warham, a Charleston cabinetmaker, advertised in 1734 that he made bookcases, and Rouland Baughan's estate inventory of 22 November 1736 listed "1 mehogany bookcase with 16 square glasses £20." On 10 June 1771 a notice concerning the auction of Thomas Shirley's household furniture mentioned "*A Mahogany Library Case* with eight doors, four above and four below, is nine Feet two-inches high, and seven feet wide, has a scroll Pediment Head with dentiled Cornice and Frize; is in nine Pieces for the Convenience of moving, and fixed together with Screws." According to Thomas Elfe's account book, he sold John Dart a "library bookcase with Chinese Doors and drawers under them £100" in 1772. *Acc. 949.*

FA

35 Library bookcase from Chippendale, *The Gentleman and Cabinet Maker's Director*, Second Ed., 1759. *Acc. 2645.*

36

Rachel Moore Allston, oil on canvas, by Henry Benbridge, Charleston, 1784. Henry Benbridge was born in Philadelphia in 1743 and was educated by his stepfather, Thomas Gordon. He may have been instructed by John Wollaston, who painted Gordon's portrait, for some of Benbridge's early portraits reflect Wollaston's style; he may also have trained briefly under Matthew Pratt. By 1765 Benbridge was studying in Rome with Pompeo Battoni and perhaps Anton Mengs; before that period, he is thought to have spent a short time in London under the tutelage of Benjamin West, who referred him to Battoni and Mengs. Benbridge returned to America in the 1770s, and in 1772 he moved to Charleston. Except for a two-year absence in the 1780s, he remained in Charleston painting and teaching—Thomas Coram was one of his students—until the 1790s, when he moved to Norfolk. He died on 25 January 1813 and was buried at Christ Church in Philadelphia.

Benbridge's Italian training in the continental and Neoclassical styles is reflected in his later portraits. He favored colors such as brilliant yellow gold, deep rich reds, and the rich blue of this portrait. He often painted his subjects in outdoor settings with classical columns, parklike vistas, and ornamental foliage. He used glazes, another Italian technique; the delicate coloring of Mrs. Allston's forehead, throat, and hand were created in this manner. Benbridge also was drawn to the conversational form of portraiture.

Rachel Moore Allston (1757–1839) was the daughter of John and Elizabeth Vanderhorst Moore. She married William Allston, Jr., in 1775 and lived with him on his Waccamaw River plantation near Pawley's Island until his death. In 1784 she married Rhode Island native Henry Collins Flagg. The artist Washington Allston (44) was her second son by her first marriage. *Acc. 2023-11.*   *FA*

37 Unknown family portrait, oil on canvas, Henry Benbridge, Charleston, 1780–90. This painting is in the style of conversational portraiture made fashionable in England by Arthur Devis and John Zoffany. These paintings usually portrayed group subjects, either families or friends, in indoor or outdoor settings relating to the group in some way and in attitudes suggesting that the subjects were conversing. In general, the artists paid great attention to foreground and background detail, as well as forms and modes of dress. Although this form of painting was widely espoused in England, Benbridge and his friend Charles Willson Peale were the only artists working in the South to try their hands at it.

This portrait of an unknown Charleston family basically follows the "conversation" format. The subjects are placed in an outdoor setting rich in foliage and arranged in a manner that suggests an interchange between the two. Most notable are the rifle, a rarity in early Low Country portraits, and the small figures and oversized heads of the subjects, a style Benbridge apparently adopted from his acquaintance with Thomas Patch, another English artist noted for his conversation pieces and caricatures. Some of the works of other English conversationalists, such as George Stubbs and Zoffany, also verge on caricatures, although not as noticeably as Patch's.

This portrait descended in the Roux and Poinsett families of Charleston and Georgetown, South Carolina, respectively, and it is possible that the subjects were members of one of these families.

Gift of Mr. and Mrs. Thomas Douglas III, acc. 3263.

FA

38 Card table, Charleston, 1770–80. Late Rococo furniture styles in Charleston are often described as Neoclassical, but instead they demonstrate an early Neoclassical influence on Rococo forms. By the late 1760s and early 1770s panels of book-matched crotch veneer edged with stringing, inlaid husks, and serpentine forms were increasingly apparent on tables and case furniture made in the city, often showing a blend of British, French, and even German stylistic influence. An example of this large group of transitional objects, this card table has the "canted" legs typical of late Rococo Charleston work. Elfe charged John Gaillard in 1773 for "two commode card tables"; based on that description, they were probably of this shape. The most imposing example of this group of inlaid Charleston Rococo furniture is a library bookcase made about 1770 for John Edwards, whose 1781 inventory described "A Large Mahogany Book Case £100.00.00." It is on display in the Heyward-Washington house, a property of the Charleston Museum. *Acc. 1185.* *JB*

39 Armchair, Wilmington, North Carolina, 1770–85. Although it is situated over 150 miles up the coast from Charleston, the Cape Fear region of North Carolina often is considered to be an extension of the Low Country. Among the Charleston cabinetmakers who emigrated to Wilmington, the Cape Fear's principal city, was John Nutt, who was working in Wilmington by 1771 and died in 1811 after a prosperous career. This mahogany armchair, one of a set of at least fourteen chairs, descended from George Elliot, a Scot who settled near Fayetteville in Cumberland County, North Carolina, during the late Revolutionary period. In addition to the chairs remaining from this set, two other chairs from the same shop have been recorded, each with different splat and crest patterns. All are of mahogany, but the greater difficulty of obtaining that wood in North Carolina is evident in the very thin seat rails used by this chairmaker.
Gift of Mr. and Mrs. George London, acc. 3590. *JB*

40 *Charles Paxton Butler*, oil on canvas, by James Earl, Charleston, 1794–96. James Earl, the younger brother of New England artist Ralph Earl, was born in 1761. In 1784 he went to London, where he remained for ten years, studying with Benjamin West and John Singleton Copley and exhibiting at the Royal Academy. On his return to America in 1794, his ship was blown off course and he landed in Charleston, where he spent two years painting portraits. He died in 1796. His obituary in the *South Carolina State Gazette* of 18 August 1796 characterized his work, which shows the influence of West, Copley, and his brother, fairly aptly: "To an uncommon facility in hitting off the likeness, may be added a peculiarity in his execution of drapery, and, which has ever been esteemed in his art the *ne plus ultra* of giving life to the eye and expression to every feature."

Charles Paxton Butler, born in Boston in 1765, was listed as a silversmith in the Charleston city directories from 1790 to 1829. In 1798 he married Mrs. Ann Poyas, and he died in 1858. *Acc. 2023-38.*

FA

41 *The Cart Children*, oil on canvas, attributed to Thomas Coram, Charleston, 1802–3. The attribution of this work to Coram is based on its similarities to his signed portrait of Mrs. Thomas Glover, also in the MESDA collection, and his religious painting *Jesus Said Suffer Little Children*, now in the collection of the South Carolina Society. Coram was born in England and arrived in Charleston in 1769. He advertised as an engraver in the 1770s and 1780s and was identified as such in early Charleston directories. He died in 1811. According to the Charleston miniaturist Charles Fraser, Coram stud-ied painting with Henry Benbridge (36, 37). This painting supports that statement, for certain elements, notably the little boy, are similar to those of Henry Benbridge's painting *The Four Generations*.

The children in this portrait, Christopher and Suzanna Cart, died young, in 1800 and 1801, respectively, and it is believed that Coram painted them after their deaths. Their father, John Cart, was a friend of Coram's.

James G. Hanes Memorial Fund in memory of P. Huber Hanes, Jr., acc. 2672. FA

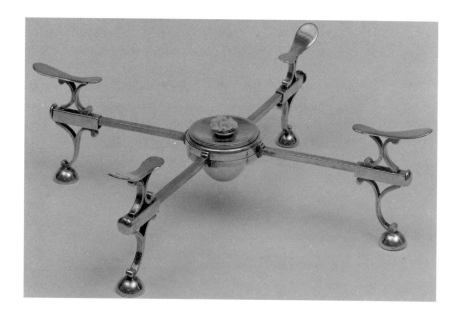

42

Dish cross, by Christian Charles Lewis Wittich, Charleston, 1795–1805. Charleston, unlike southern coastal cities north of the Low Country, had a substantial German element. Charles Wittich, a German emigrant, was first listed in a city directory in 1794 at a location on Meeting Street; he later occupied various addresses on Broad Street. Like most Charleston silversmiths of the late eighteenth century, Wittich imported extensively. He advertised in October 1800 that he had just received "from London, as large and elegant an assortment of Jewellry and Fancy Articles, GOLD, GILT, AND PLATED, As was ever offered for sale in this city." The assortment included a wide variety of objects, and among the "plated articles" listed were "Dish Crosses, with and without lamps." The dish cross illustrated here is not plated, but it is fitted with a spirit lamp. American dish crosses are rare; that this one is a product of Wittich's shop and not an import is indicated by the marks. Each foot is struck four times on the bottom with Wittich's "CW" mark, and since the bottoms of the domed feet were a separate piece of sheet silver, the marks were struck before the feet were brazed together.

Wittich formed a partnership with his brother Frederick in 1802. The partnership was dissolved in 1806, and the following year Wittich advertised that he was "about to decline business, and to leave Charleston." He may have been working as late as 1811, however, since he is described as a "goldsmith" in an estate settlement of that year. *Acc. 2861.*   JB

43

Saucepan, by Nathaniel Vernon, Charleston, 1800–1810. Vernon worked in Charleston from about 1801 until at least 1835, even though in 1820 he advertised that he wished to "decline" his business and "dispose of his whole establishment," including his house and lot on Broad near the corner of King Street. Most of Vernon's advertisements list extensive arrays of imported ware, but he occasionally advertised that "every kind of Gold and Silver Work, Hair Work, Engraving, &c." would be "executed in the best manner" in his shop. A notice in 1810 proudly announced that Vernon had employed "an Artist of the first rate ability" that could execute "any article in Gold and Silver . . . equal to that which is imported from Europe." The small saucepan illustrated here bears the touch "N. VERNON," and very likely was made to be used with a spirit lamp and stand. *Acc. 2473.*   JB

44 *A Rocky Coast with Banditti*, oil on canvas, by
Washington Allston, Charleston, 1800. Born in 1779
to William and Rachel Moore Allston (36) of
coastal South Carolina, Washington Allston was
America's first full-scale romantic artist. He was
educated in Newport, Rhode Island, and at Har-
vard. He settled briefly in Charleston after graduat-
ing in 1800, and in 1801 sailed to England with his
friend Edward Greene Malbone, the miniaturist.
He remained abroad, chiefly in England, for seventeen years, and was elected an associate of the
Royal Academy. He returned to the United States
in 1818 and took up residence in the North. He
died in 1843.

Allston influenced a number of nineteenth-cen-
tury English and American artists, among them
Samuel F. B. Morse. Allston painted mostly landscapes and classical and biblical scenes and narra-
tives; his portraits are few. This landscape, one of
his earliest, demonstrates his early interest in the
romantic style. Signed and dated by Allston, it was
exhibited in the British Institution at Somerset
House in London in 1802 with two other landscapes, now lost. *Acc. 2098.*   FA

45
Sideboard, coastal South Carolina, 1800–1810. Made of mahogany, mahogany veneer, poplar, and yellow pine, this six-leg Neoclassical sideboard has quarter-shaped ends, indented doors under a long center drawer, and rectangular and oval panels of light wood and husk stringing on its legs. Its center drawer also has an outset panel with a fan patera at the center; fans were a popular inlay motif in Charleston, appearing more frequently on Pembroke tables than sideboards.

This sideboard has a Georgetown, South Carolina, area history, and it is one of three recorded as having a coastal South Carolina rather than a Charleston provenance. All three resemble each other slightly in the manner of drawer construction and inlay design, but this example is the only one with quarter-shaped ends. One of the others descended in a Berkeley County family. Although it lacks the fans and bellflowers of MESDA's example, its leg panels, stringing, and construction features are similar. *Acc. 950-5.* FA

46
Secretary and bookcase, Wilmington, North Carolina, 1795–1815. The influence of northern cabinet-making centers on the coastal South is quite evident in this mahogany secretary, which in both form and style closely follows work attributable to Boston and Salem in Massachusetts. The form of the pediment, the latticed tracery of the bookcase doors, and the deployment of a three-drawer carcass over tall, tapering legs are Massachusetts details, as are all of the four varieties of elaborate string inlay. Boston, like New York, was an export center for highly specialized work such as inlay. It is entirely possible that a Massachusetts cabinet-maker moved to the Cape Fear and maintained his sources of supply in Boston. The unusual vine-and-leaf inlay of the tympanum, however, has nothing to do with the Boston/Salem style. It is a regional detail that is parallel to similar work in Norfolk, another port city heavily influenced by New England styles during the Neoclassical period and even before.

Gift of Mrs. Thomas L. Chatham, acc. 3279. JB

47

Desk, Wilmington, North Carolina, 1795–1805. The small size of this mahogany desk makes it tempting to identify it as a "ladies'" desk, but there is evidence that both sexes commonly used small desks during the Neoclassical period. An unusual retention from the Baroque period is the stepped interior drawers. A single wide drawer is fitted just below the fallboard. The use of unpinned mortise-and-tenon joints at the junctures of the legs and frame is an urban detail. Another desk from the same shop, identical in almost every detail, has a history of ownership in Bladen County, which is located up the Cape Fear River from Wilmington. *Acc. 2023-30.* *JB*

48 Armchair, Charleston, 1790–1800. This mahogany armchair with cypress braces and ash and yellow pine seat rails is one of a pair in the MESDA collection and originally was part of a set of twelve that descended in the Ball family of Charleston. Its shield back carved with drapery swags and plumes is a form usually associated with late-eighteenth-century New York, but we now know that this style of back was also popular in Charleston at about the same time. These armchairs differ from their New York counterparts in the construction of their seats—diagonal seat braces at each corner set with dovetail joints at the top of ash rails—and in having shortened upper arms with leaf carving. *Acc. 950-17 & 18.* FA

49 Armchair, Charleston, 1800–1810. Made of mahogany, with yellow pine corner braces and an ash seat, this Neoclassical armchair is one of a set of twelve or more dining chairs, six of which are in the MESDA collection. A similar chair is described in *The New-York Book of Prices for Cabinet and Chair Work* for 1802: "Square Back Chair, No. III With four gothic arches, and four turned columns, sweep stay, and top rail, with a brake in ditto; plain taper'd legs." Several New York examples in various collections have been attributed to the shop of partners Abraham Slover and Jacob Taylor, who worked in New York City from 1802 to 1805. This armchair resembles these New York products, but it lacks their four corner rosettes and its upper panel is carved with thirteen flutes rather than the sunbursts and swags popular in the North. Like the arms of the Charleston shield-back chairs (48) in the MESDA collection, those of this chair are shorter than their New York counterparts. *Acc. 2237-1.* FA

50 Pembroke table, by James Main, Charleston, 1813–22. The strong New York City details on this table, such as the reeded edge of the shaped top and the inverted vase form of the feet, lead us to suspect that the maker was trained in the North, but this has not been documented. New York details on Charleston case furniture, beds, and tables are common. James Main, who scrawled his name in chalk on the cypress drawer bottom of this table, is first listed in Charleston directories in 1813; the last recorded listing for him was at 63 Broad Street in 1822. He appears to have enjoyed a brisk trade, for in 1817 he advertised for "A FEW *Journeymen Cabinet Makers*, whose labor will be punctually paid." No advertisements for his work have been found, very likely another indication of success, for artisans with ample custom had little need to advertise. *Acc. 2496.* JB

51 Pair of andirons, England, 1785–1810. Before the Revolution, relatively little American brass was produced: England did not permit the export of zinc or brass ingot to the colonies, and copper mines were not exploited in this country until the last quarter of the century. After 1783, however, by which time England had become a coal-burning country, American brassfounders became leading manufacturers of andirons. Regional American styles, particularly those of Boston, New York, and Philadelphia, have been identified. It was once thought that Charleston was the only southern city that produced andirons with a recognizable regional style, but recent research has revealed that these were not made in Charleston, but apparently were manufactured for the Charleston market in England and exported to that port city. A prodigious number have been recorded, and it is possible that some were copied in Charleston from the English originals. Those illustrated here, with their obelisk-like pillars and arched feet ornamented with a pair of intersecting scrolls, are early examples and probably are English. *Acc. 3799.* FA

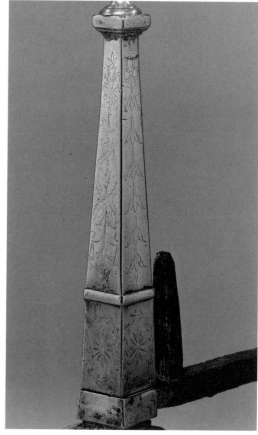

52

Fireback, by the Charleston Iron Foundry, 1802–22. Castings such as this normally were produced by merchant furnaces in Virginia, Maryland, and Pennsylvania; however, some were the work of foundries—or "air furnaces," as they were called—that operated in various port towns during the eighteenth and nineteenth centuries. Unlike a full-scale blast furnace, a foundry operation was essentially a large version of a blacksmith's forge used to melt commercial pig iron for running hollow ware and other such objects. In 1802 John Johnson, a Charleston blacksmith, built "an air furnace about four miles" from Charleston on the Cooper River. A Baltimore newspaper account of that year reported that Johnson was producing cast-iron objects "equal in neatness and lightness to any that have been brought to" Charleston, and that among other things he produced "chimney-backs." The foundry was sold to the firm of Brodie and Evans in 1822. *Acc. 2997.*　　　　　*JB*

53

William Trenholm, watercolor on ivory miniature, attributed to Edward Greene Malbone, Charleston, 1800–1805. Edward Greene Malbone is probably America's best-known miniature painter. He was born in Newport, Rhode Island, in 1777 and began his career in Providence in 1794. From 1794 to 1807 he worked in Providence, Newport, Boston, New York, Philadelphia, Charleston, and Savannah, turning out a great many miniatures. In 1801 he traveled to England for a short visit in the company of his friend Washington Allston. In 1806 he went to Jamaica for health reasons; he returned to Savannah in January 1807 and died on 7 May of that year.

William Trenholm was born in Charleston in 1772, married in 1803, and died on the coast of Africa of yellow fever. This miniature is still in its original frame, the back of which contains the owner's gold initials and braided hairwork. *Acc. 2776-2.*　　　　　*FA*

54 *Mrs. John Ball, Jr.*, oil on canvas, attributed to Samuel Finley Breese Morse, Charleston, 1818–22. Samuel F. B. Morse was born in Charlestown, Massachusetts, in 1791. Although he is probably best known for his work with the telegraph, Morse began his career painting portraits while at Yale University. In 1811 he traveled to London to study with his friend Washington Allston at the Royal Academy under Benjamin West, and in 1815 he returned to the United States. From 1818 to 1822 he spent several winters in Charleston painting portraits. He settled in New York in 1823 and died there in 1872.

Mrs. John Ball, Jr., née Ann Simons, lived on Comingtee Plantation, thirty miles above Charleston. *Acc. 2108.* FA

The Backcountry

Even early in the settlement of the southern tidewater, adventurous folk were preoccupied with the vast region lying far to the west of the coast. John Lawson undertook a long and dangerous exploration of the North Carolina piedmont early in the eighteenth century, describing the land at the foot of the mountains as "the most noble and sweetest Part of this Country . . . not inhabited by any but the Savages." This was to change rapidly after the 1740s. In 1772 Peter Manigault, after returning from a long sojourn into the piedmont, wrote that "the back parts of the Province have settled extremely fast, insomuch, that it is computed that there have been at least 10,000 White Inhabitants come in from the Northern Colonies in one Year only. They all travelled by Land, so that We upon the Sea Coast did not perceive with what Rapidity [the] Colony was increasing."

Spilling down the Great Wagon Road that traversed the Shenandoah Valley of Virginia, the enormous flood of new settlers had inundated the northern Valley by the 1730s and had reached the Yadkin River valley of North Carolina before the end of the 1740s. From Virginia and North Carolina they spread out to South Carolina, Tennessee, and Kentucky. A correspondent in Kentucky wrote in 1786 that "it will be as practicable to turn a torrent of water backward, as to prevent the amazing emigration to this country . . . they are of all nations, tongues and languages, from our own country, and every part of Europe they are gathered."

Although the Chesapeake and the Low Country housed many immigrants from Europe, and some made a significant impact in the arts, as the French certainly did in Charleston, coastal settlement patterns contrasted greatly with those west of the fall line. The coastal South, as we have seen through the eyes of visitors and in the objects made by coastal artisans, was forthrightly British. Not so the Backcountry, a potpourri of national cultures, which produced the most complex and extensive blending of ethnic styles the new country had seen since the beginning of the seventeenth century.

In Europe and Britain the massive outward migration that led to the creation of the Backcountry had begun in the early seventeenth century. The Presbyterian lowland Scots transported to Northern Ireland early in the century were soon harassed by the Anglican High Church party and were denied both civil and religious rights under the Test Act of 1704. Outrageous feudal quitrents, a failing economy, and the famine of the 1720s drove the Scots-Irish to America; 6,000 settled in Pennsylvania in 1729 alone. Germans and Swiss fared no better in their homeland. Long residents of an international buffer zone, the peasants of the Rhenish Palatinate suffered during the 1688–97 War of the League of Augsburg and then during the War of Spanish Succession, which began in 1702. Before the conflict ended in 1714, Catholics had been set against Protestants, Bourbons against Hapsburgs, and the shifting alliances of the war put the German states in conflict with each other as well. The Rhine Valley was devastated by the armies of Louis XIV, and by 1708 shiploads of German immigrants were arriving daily in Philadelphia. French Huguenots, who fled the Continent in great numbers after the Revocation of the Edict of Nantes in 1685, found their way to the American coast as well as the Backcountry.

Highland Scots, who had suffered extensively at the hands of the English, were given leave to emigrate to America after the bloody Battle of Culloden in 1746. Most of them—in contrast to the bulk of Backcountry settlers, who came from the North—poured up the rivers from the coast, moving as far west as Tennessee. English Quakers, who had suffered oppression in both Britain and the colonies, began an extensive settlement of the piedmont after 1750. In northeastern North Carolina, where the Quakers had become quietly dominant in politics, the Anglican priest John Urmstone described them as "very numerous . . . insufferably proud, and consequently ungovernable."

In actuality the Quakers and Germans were the best-ordered settlers of the Backcountry. They congregated in their own settlements, the Germans pushing well toward the mountains. Beginning with Jost Hite's settlement at Massanutten in the Shenandoah Valley, the German settlers in particular became known for their efficient farming, husbandry, and trade. The Moravians,

Piedmont room, Guilford County, North Carolina, c. 1766.

McLean House exterior, Guilford County, North Carolina, c. 1766.

who had established the earliest German Protestant church, in 1753 leased 100,000 acres of land in North Carolina from agents of Lord Granville. By 1770 Wachovia, as their settlement was called, had three towns inhabited by some of the most skilled tradesmen in the Backcountry, many of them trained in Europe. The Moravians were known as a "people remarkable for their orderly behavior, plain obliging manners, unvaried economy, and a steady unremitting industry." Other German settlers in the Backcountry had much the same reputation.

Then there were the people that someone in Winchester, Virginia, described in 1755 as "a spurious race of mortals known by the appellation of Scotch-Irish." Also incorrectly called simply "Irish," these settlers were restless, rugged individualists fiercely determined to do with the land as they pleased after a century and a half of oppression in Ulster. They cared little for the tidewater

Catawba bedroom, Catawba County, North Carolina, c. 1811.

Catawba House exterior, Catawba County, North Carolina, c. 1811.

politics that represented the presence of the Crown in the South and shunned representatives of the government. In 1749 several inhabitants of Morgan Bryan's settlement on the Yadkin River in North Carolina were hauled into court for threatening a surveyor "by drawing the Swords on him and threatening to shoot him with Rifles." Two years later the Bryan settlement welcomed another family, the Boones, from Bucks County, Pennsylvania, among them young Daniel Boone, a man destined to leave an indelible impression on the frontier. The Scots-Irish were in the vanguard of Backcountry settlers, in many cases buying up the best parcels of land—usually in blocks of 640 acres, or a square mile—for land on the frontier was cheap. These settlers were the nucleus of the groundswell of sentiment for independence during the last decade of the colonial period, and they proved to be fierce patriots.

The awesome expanse of the southern Backcountry,

Catawba hall, or parlor, Catawba County, North Carolina, c. 1811.

geographically split by the Appalachians and a system of deep rivers, was scarcely governable until after the Revolution. The population rose sharply after about 1730. North Carolina's whole population was scarcely more than 30,000 in 1730, but on the eve of the Revolution the white population alone had risen to 265,000, more than half of them in the piedmont. In Maryland, Virginia, and South Carolina the coastal regions retained not only the seats of government but dominance in commerce as well. By contrast, North Carolina's vital force shifted to the interior.

The entire Backcountry, including Tennessee and Kentucky after the Indian problems were solved, became a huge melting pot of national and international styles in the arts. British furniture forms were adopted by German artisans and decorated in regional styles from a dozen German states. Scots-Irish and German cabinet-makers alike brought a flood of stylistic details from the imposing Delaware Valley style, which centered upon Philadelphia. Backcountry potters learned to fashion earthenware in the Staffordshire style, adding urban styles to ancient traditions of colorful slip-decorated peasant wares. Backcountry furnaces—the largest southern industry short of shipbuilding—shrewdly offered cast iron in any style preferred by their customers, jamb stoves covered with Biblical scenes for Germans, elegant parlor stoves for English customers. A factor as important as the diversity of ethnic groups in encouraging the strong development of vibrant regional styles was the Backcountry's relative isolation, caused by its great distance from urban design centers. Some Backcountry styles were almost urban in quality. Others were colorfully naive, in considerable contrast to the formal elegance of the coastal regions.

1 Armchair, Shenandoah Valley of Virginia, 1740–70. The earliest furniture forms of the southern Backcountry usually are associated with German settlements, thanks to the Germanic tendency to cling to early styles. This chair essentially has a Renaissance form. In style and construction, including the wainscot back molded only at the edges of the central stile, the plank seat, and the sloping arms, it is similar to seventeenth-century wainscot chairs made in New England. The later date of this chair, however, is evident in its thin stretchers and seat rails, its relatively delicate front legs, the lack of architectural form in its turnings, and its very plain crest rail. The use of pairs of stretchers on both the front and sides of the chair is related more to the post-and-round, or "ladderback," tradition than to the usual form of wainscot chairs.

Several other chairs of this type with a Shenandoah Valley provenance have been recorded, at least one with an open back composed of straight balusters. Similar chairs were produced in the German settlements of southeastern Pennsylvania, but many of those have a heavier construction that lends them an earlier appearance. The MESDA chair is walnut throughout, whereas American coastal wainscot chairs of the seventeenth century were made of oak. It was found near Lexington, Virginia, in the southern portion of the Valley, but probably was made in the area between Augusta and Shenandoah counties. *Acc. 2026.* *JB*

2 Stretcher table, central piedmont North Carolina, 1755–85. It is difficult to assign precise dates to German-American furniture. This cherry table, with its massive legs, has a very early appearance, but the lack of dovetailed battens for attaching the top to the frame and the absence of a molding at the bottom edges of the frame members suggest a later date. The turnings, similar in details to linen wheels made well into the nineteenth century, are in a vernacular style more appropriate to a wheelwright than a turner. Wheelwrights in the piedmont South often produced spinning wheels, many of them signed and dated.

Gift of Mr. and Mrs. Ralph P. Hanes, acc. 1072. *JB*

Five decorated chests. In the first decade of the eighteenth century, German Palatine immigrants settling in the western fringes of Philadelphia were introduced to British furniture forms prevalent in that city. By the mid-eighteenth century, the British impact on German-American furniture was well established. Chests were a familiar form in Germanic Europe, but there they tended to retain Renaissance detail with massive architectural bases and profuse paneling. Pennsylvania-German cabinetmakers adopted the lighter lid and base moldings, as well as the bracket feet, typical of British case furniture.

Painted decoration was popular in rural regions of most European countries and therefore often is considered to be peasant art; however, it is found on sophisticated urban work as well. The Frederick, Maryland, chest (3, below left) shown here is inscribed with its original owner's name, Adam Neff, and the date 1791. Its decoration was executed with a very unusual technique. The design was incised through a coat of deep green to reveal an orange base color underneath, much in the manner of sgraffito decoration on earthenware. Another chest by this artist, also with a Frederick provenance, is known. *Acc. 2738.*

Most surviving southern furniture with painted decoration is from western Virginia. In that region, such furniture was understood to be "Dutch," that is, *Deutsch*, or German; the 1793 appraisal of the estate of Gasper Enders of Frederick County included "2 German Chests £0:17:6." Perhaps the best-known Shenandoah Valley decorator is Johannes Spitler (1774–1837) of Shenandoah County. An impressive series of chests and two tall clock cases bearing his decoration have been recorded. Spitler's work is highly individualistic and readily recognizable. Most of his designs were compass-drawn, which is not unusual for American decorated chests, but his patterns generally are unlike most Pennsylvania work. The joinery of the chests bearing Spitler's decoration is consistent, suggesting the possibility that he made the furniture as well as decorating it, but this has not been documented. MESDA's chest (4, below right) is of yellow pine throughout and may be dated 1795–1810. *Ann Bahnson Gray Purchase Fund, acc. 3806.*

Virginia's most extensive school of decorated furniture is associated with Wythe County in the southwestern part of the state. A community of Germans and Swiss settled in the western half of the county and by 1800 had established four Lutheran and Reformed churches, all within a ten-mile radius. Four distinct groups of Wythe chests have been identified, most of them with three painted arched-head panels containing pots of tu-

lips and other lacy, tuliplike flowers. Later examples have lunetted panels such as those on a MESDA chest (5, top right) of 1820–30. Two chests bear a signature thought to be that of Johannes Hudel or Huddle (1772–1839), suggesting the possibility that the Huddle family may have been responsible for the decoration and possibly the joinery of many of these chests. The MESDA example, like many others from this school, is entirely of poplar. *Acc. 4009.*

Decorated chests from North Carolina are rare. An 1800–1815 example at MESDA (6, right) is attributed to Alamance County in the piedmont, based on the provenance of a plain walnut chest and a walnut chest of drawers by the same cabinetmaker who made MESDA's chest. Another decorated chest from the same shop has been recorded, suggesting that in this case the cabinetmaker probably was the decorator as well. All the drawer and carcass dovetails of this group of furniture are wedged, a common Germanic construction detail. Each dovetail pin was cut in the center with a thin-bladed saw, and wedges were driven into these saw kerfs after the drawer was assembled, thereby tightening each joint. A German settlement was located in the Alamance area by the 1740s, but very little is known about it. A particularly interesting detail used by this decorator is the bands of painted lozenges, which resemble Neoclassical inlay. *Acc. 789.*

Also from the North Carolina piedmont and attributed to the area of Chatham or Randolph County is a yellow pine chest (7, below) dated 1801. It is one of several pieces of furniture known to have been decorated by the same hand; a table bears the initials "NY," probably those of an owner. This chest, unlike the preceding examples, owes nothing to the Germanic tradition; its decoration style is far more British. The brushwork used to execute the spread-winged eagle, as well as the extensive border work, is reminiscent of the single-stroke brushwork of decorated tinware, better known as "tole." Under the black base color of this chest is a light coat of red primer. *Acc. 2528.*   JB

8 Tall clock, Rowan County, North Carolina, 1805–
15. The inlay on the walnut case of this clock shows
British influence in the use of segmental fanlike
motifs, and the general form of the case and inset
quarter columns are related, if distantly, to Delaware Valley work. The fanciful folk motifs, including the face in the tympanum, the sun piercing a
quarter moon in the waist door—suggesting an
allusion to the sun overcoming darkness—and the
bicolored "fylfot" at the bottom of the door, argue
strongly for a German cabinetmaker. The clock
descended in the prominent Steierwalt (Stirewalt)
family of housewrights. Several houses attributed
to John and Jacob Stirewalt still stand in Rowan
County.

The brass thirty-hour clock works are attributed
to piedmont North Carolina's most prolific clockmaker, Johann Ludwig Eberhardt, who arrived
in the Moravian town of Salem, North Carolina,
from Germany in 1799 and worked there until 1837.
Salem is located about forty miles northwest of
the area where the Stirewalts lived. Eberhardt's
shop was inventoried in 1809 as a result of extensive
debts he had incurred; included in the inventory
were "1 8-day clock with case $60.00/ 1 30-hour
clock $30.00."

On loan to the museum, acc. 3415.   JB

Six fraktur. The term "fraktur" refers to the form of the German gothic hand, which has a "fractured" appearance. Each document had a specific purpose and name. The most commonly encountered document is the *geburts und taufschein*, or record of birth and baptism, frequently known simply as a *taufschein*. Rarer fraktur documents included such things as the *haus segen*, or house blessing, and the *vorschrift*, or letter exercise. Although the term originated with the illuminated manuscripts whose heritage lay in the calligraphy and illustration practiced in medieval monasteries, by the seventeenth century fraktur had become the art of the people, notably in the Rhenish Palatinate south into Switzerland. Although gaily decorated, the documents were intended primarily as records, and most were not displayed as decoration. Like these examples, virtually all fraktur are ink and watercolor on paper.

The *taufschein* of Scharlotta (Charlotte) Meier (9, right) records her birth on 13 January 1783. The location is not listed but is thought to have been Frederick County, Maryland. Like many of the more elaborate and large *taufscheine*, this example is covered with a good deal of religious text in addition to the basic information about the birth and baptism of the child and the names of *taufzeugen*, or witnesses. The birth or even the baptism date listed on a *taufschein* is no proof of the date that the document was executed, for many were drawn later. The style of this *taufschein* suggests a probable date in the 1780s; the vertical format was employed more frequently after about 1790. *Gift of William H. Petree, acc. 2801.*

Georg Miller was born on 16 March 1786 in "Schenandoah Caunty," as his *taufschein* (10, below) records. The artist who rendered the document was the anonymous "Stony Creek" artist, so named for the region of Shenandoah County where he worked during the late eighteenth century. Numerous examples of his (or her) work have been recorded, some of them in English, which is unusual for *taufscheine* drawn for German families. Characteristic of this artist's work are the ruled borders filled with running leafage and tulips on vines. Particularly typical of this group is a fringed "heavenly curtain" suspended from the two upper corners of the border, a detail not used on this document. *Mr. and Mrs. James R. Melchor Purchase Fund, acc. 3853.*

Fraktur by definition is German, but the close proximity of different ethnic groups in one region brought about cross-linked styles in many of the arts. Birth and memorial documents by an anonymous Virginia "Record Book" artist who appears to have worked in Frederick County are an example of this phenomenon. Bordering Frederick on the south was Shenandoah County, where the "Stony Creek" artist was located, and it is interesting to observe that both artists used similar ruled borders with fleurs-de-lis in the corners. But the "Record Book" artist—so-called because much of his work is bound into ledgerlike volumes—probably was not a German, and none of his work is in the fraktur hand. The background of a number of his patrons suggests that he was a Scots-Irish Presbyterian. Characteristic of this artist are a curtainlike motif inside the central blocks (not unlike the "heavenly curtain" of the "Stony Creek" artist), an elaborate bird, sinuous calligraphic flourishes filling the borders, and flowers, all of which appear on the birth and death records for Anna Hott (11, left and below left). *Acc. 3915-1 & 2.*

One of the most prolific fraktur artists in the Shenandoah Valley was Peter Bernhardt of Keezletown in Rockingham County, who advertised in the *Winchester Gazette* in 1789 that he had "commenced the business of riding as Post from Winchester to Staunton." Bernhardt's style was heavily influenced by the work of Friedrich Krebs, a well-known fraktur artist of Dauphin County, Pennsylvania. One Krebs *taufschein* form was filled in by Bernhardt, which is not unusual since artists commonly made up blank but ornamented forms to be completed later. Bernhardt himself had a long association with the printer Ambrose Henkel of New Market, who printed standard forms for the artist. The *taufschein* of Friederich Steierwalt (12, next page, above) was drawn by Bernhardt, signed by the artist, and dated 1808. The German script text was left blank and the document sent to Rowan County, North Carolina, where it was filled in. Characteristic of Bernhardt's work are the "popeyed" birds perched on a tall plant with strange bacteria-like blooms. *On loan to the museum, acc. 3416-1.*

Even though the German settlements of piedmont North Carolina were extensive, relatively little remains of the arts produced in these settlements, the Moravian communities excepted. North Carolina fraktur is particularly rare. One of two *taufscheine* done for the Stirewalt family, the 1800–1810 document for Johannes Steierwalt (13, next page, below), records that the child was baptized "in der Orgel Kirche," or Organ Church, a stone building that still stands. *On loan to the museum, acc. 3416-4.*

Das ver= heu mein,
Soll dir allein,
O Jesu
sein

1806 | 1825

Markz

Ist Friederich Steierwalt

Jm Jahr Chri
sti 1798 den ii ten iulius, bin ich Johañes
steier walt, auf diese iamm volle welt,
gebohren, von friedrig steier walt, und
dessen eheliche hauß frau, elster söhn,
und meine tauf zeigen, sein nemlich, Johannes steier walt,
und seine eheliche hauß frau, diese haben mich zur
heiligen tauf gebracht zu dem ehr würdigen
herr pfarren storck da dieser Gottes dienst hielt in der
orgel kirche in Rowan caundy in nort carolina
nun omeister aller zugend, Jesu lehr und führ, und führ
uns jugend, Ist führe uns auf deinen wegen, schmück
und zühre uns mit segen, laß uns wachsen in der iugend
in Gottseligkeit und zugend, und dir hier stets lob
erweisen, auch dich ewiglich dich preisen

By far the most prolific of North Carolina illuminators was the anonymous "Ehre Vater" artist, so known for his frequent use of elaborate arched "mastheads," here (14, above) urging the child to "Honor Father and Mother." It is thought that the artist may have been a parochial schoolmaster in one of the German churches in northern Davidson County. Most of his fraktur—over thirty-five documents known—were executed for Lancaster and Northampton County, Pennsylvania, subjects. His work is found as far north as Canada and has been found in the South Carolina piedmont, but the Canadian and South Carolina work almost certainly was brought in rather than done on site. The 1800–1810 *taufschein* of Maria Hege (14, above) reveals many of the standard "signatures" of the artist, including the legend at the top, the colorful female and male parakeets perched on leafy fronds, the delicate vines in the medieval style illuminating the masthead letters, and an impeccable fraktur hand. The quality of the work, coupled with the extensive use of drafting equipment, suggests that the artist may have been trained as a cartographer. *Loaned by the Archives of the Moravian Church, Southern Province, acc. 209-2.* JB

15   Jamb stove, by the Marlboro Furnace, Frederick County, Virginia, 1773–92. Although blast furnaces were operating in the southern coastal plain as early as 1622, the upper Backcountry, from western Maryland to the central Shenandoah Valley, was where such furnaces proliferated, thanks to the extensive ore beds in the mountain region and the massive limestone belt extending from Pennsylvania south to eastern Tennessee. Limestone was critical to the operation of a furnace; it was used as a flux to separate slag, or waste, from the molten iron.

All Virginia castings were run directly on the furnace floor, as the five plates of this jamb stove were. The stove is a fine representation of the juxtaposition of German culture with British, for the proprietor of the Marlboro Furnace was Isaac Zane of Philadelphia, the scion of a wealthy Quaker family. Zane operated the Marlboro works from 1767 until the early 1790s. A traditional German stove, the jamb, or "open," stove was intended for use in a *kammer*, or chamber, adjoining the *küche*, or kitchen, in a German house. Mortared into the chimney, it could be fueled from the kitchen hearth. This example bears a compelling German inscription, from Isaiah 11.6–7: "I hope for a better time when all strife shall cease [, when] cows and bears will go with each other to the pasture [and] wolves will dwell with the lambs."

St. Joe Minerals Corporation Purchase Fund, acc. 2806.   JB

16   Fireback, by the Marlboro Furnace, 1770–92. By the time that Marlboro was last put in blast, Isaac Zane owned over 35,000 acres of land, a spacious manor filled with fine furniture, and one of the largest libraries in the country. One of his neighbors was Thomas, Lord Fairfax, who shunned his princely estate in the tidewater, Belvoir, for a rural life in Frederick County. This massive fireback bears the Fairfax arms, but from the number of surviving examples it is evident that Fairfax allowed Zane to offer the castings to the general public. The source of the casting pattern has been documented by a bill from the Philadelphia carvers and gilders Bernard and Jugiez to Zane's brother-in-law, John Pemberton: "Recd. 12 moth. 1770 . . . Eight pounds for carving the Arms of Earl of Fairfax for a Pattern for the Back of Chimney sent Isaac Zane jr." *Acc. 2463.*   JB

17
Armchair, Winchester, Virginia, 1769. The emigration of Philadelphians such as Isaac Zane to the Backcountry brought about a certain demand for Philadelphia fashions, but it was the movement of the artisans themselves that ensured the dissemination of Delaware Valley furniture styles. One of a number of related chairs, this walnut example has the sculptural arms and arm supports of a Philadelphia chair in the Baroque style coupled with a Rococo splat, crest, and base. In a manner typical of Philadelphia construction, the seat rails are mortised through the back stiles. Here the development of regional style is evident in the simple carving, the molded stretchers, and the radical outward sweep of the rear legs. The chair is dated under the front seat rail. *Acc. 2428-30.* *JB*

18
Side chair, Shenandoah Valley of Virginia, 1770–1800. A Backcountry blend of national styles is amply evident in this walnut chair. The crest and base—except for the extra stretchers at the sides—reflect Chinese modes of the fifteenth century; the splat is a derivation of an early-eighteenth-century British design that also had roots in the Orient. The combined traditions of joiner and post-and-round chairmaker are demonstrated in the turned finials and feet of the front legs and also in the use of separate seat lists like those of a ladderback chair but here placed within the seat frame. This construction links the chair to other German-American chairmaking traditions, but it descended in a British family of Augusta and Stonebridge counties. *Acc. 2424.* *JB*

19

Kitchen cupboard, piedmont North Carolina, 1760–80. Like the chest, the kitchen cupboard—or *küche schrank,* as it often was listed in the inventories of German households—was freely adapted by German-Americans from a familiar rural British furniture form. The kitchen was a major room in the Germanic household, calling for a large cupboard suitable for the proud display of colorful earthenwares. This yellow pine example bears traces of its original red paint. Strongly Pennsylvania-German in the elaborate shaping of its sides and the heavy bolection moldings surrounding its cabinet doors, this cupboard has a two-piece cornice, the upper element formed by the molded edge of the top board. This detail is associated with a strong Rowan County cabinetmaking tradition.

Gift of the estate of Katherine Hanes, acc. 2073-21.

JB

20

Collection of pewter plates, Fayetteville, North Carolina (and Middletown, Connecticut), 1810–30. Displayed in the kitchen cupboard are twenty-two pewter plates, most of them by three Middletown, Connecticut, pewterers, Jacob Eggleston, Jehiel Johnson, and William Nott. These men formed something of a pewterers' consortium in their complex partnerships and constant travel between Connecticut and North Carolina. All three men were engaged in business together at one time or another and with other partners as well, making Fayetteville virtually the only southern center noted for an extensive pewterer's trade. Eggleston (1773–1813) and Johnson (c. 1785–1833) both died in Middletown; Nott (1789–c. 1840) was in Fayetteville at the time of his death.

Middletown hosted a large contingent of pewterers, including prominent families such as the Danforths. Nott advertised in 1809 that he had "taken the shop belonging to Mr. William Danforth." One of his partners in Fayetteville was Joseph Sumner, a tinsmith; the firm established a "Tin and Sheet Iron Ware Manufactory . . . South of the Market" in 1829. Eggleston had a similar partnership with Daniel Bass, a tinsmith from Berlin, Connecticut. In 1807 the firm announced that they had "commenced the Tin Plate Working, Pewter and Copper Smiths Business" in Fayetteville.

It is probable that at least some of the pewter sold by these men in North Carolina was made in Connecticut. A plate in the collection by James Martine includes in the mark "FAYT. N.C," the only plate with a Carolina address. The marks of the other Fayetteville artisans all contain an eagle, popular among Middletown pewterers. One of Eggleston's marks, in fact, appears to have been cut by the same engraver that made one of William Danforth's early dies. Martine, like many pewterers, carried on other trades as well, advertising his "Copper, Tin and Sheet Iron" manufactory on Hay Street in 1829.

The collection is the gift of Mr. and Mrs. Ralph P. Hanes, with two exceptions: one Johnson plate, donated by the estate of Katherine Hanes, and the Martine plate, donated by Mrs. W. I. Brooks, acc. 586, 2070, 2073-13 & 14, 2404.　　　　　　　　*JB*

21

Pokal, lead glass, engraved "F. Marshall," by John Frederick Amelung, Frederick County, Maryland, 1785–92. It is believed that this large crystal covered goblet, or pokal, was presented to Frederick William Marshall, the Moravian administrator of Wachovia, by his daughter and granddaughter. Aennel von Marshall and Johanna Elizabeth von Schweintz traveled overland from Pennsylvania to Salem in 1792, and if they took the usual route, they would have passed through Frederick County, Maryland.

John Frederick Amelung, a native of Bremen, Germany, established the New Bremen Glass Manufactory in Frederick County in 1784 and operated it until 1795. He is the only eighteenth-century American glass manufacturer whose products can be identified. In 1785 he advertised in the *Maryland Journal and Baltimore Advertiser* that he made "all kinds of Glass-Wares, viz. Window-Glass, from the lowest to the finest sorts, white and green Bottles, Wine and other Drinking-Glasses, finished compleat." He is known to have presented George Washington with two goblets.

Loaned by the Wachoria Historical Society, acc. G-105. FA

22

Sugar bowl, clear glass, attributed to the New Bremen Glass Manufactory, Frederick County, Maryland, 1785–95. The attribution of this clear, non-lead glass sugar bowl is based on its design. The applied ring supporting the top and the finial in particular, features seen on other attributed pieces, are considered Amelung characteristics.

Gift of Thomas A. Gray, acc. 3192. FA

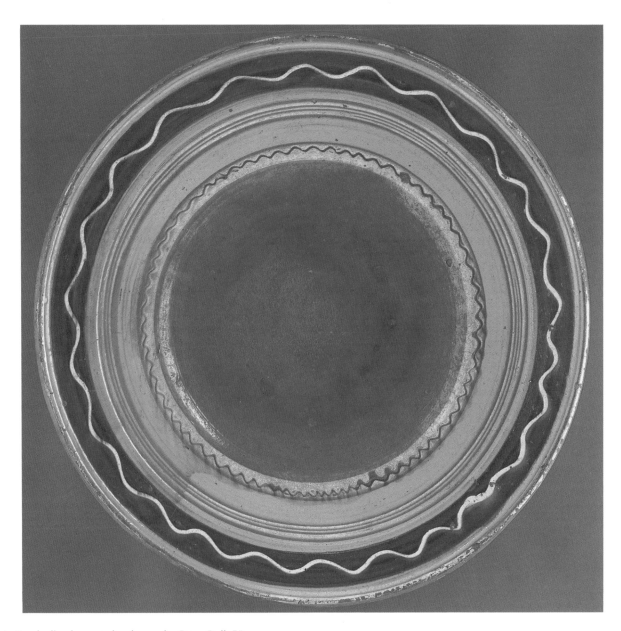

23

Bowl, slip-decorated redware, by Peter Bell, Hagerstown, Maryland, 1805–10. The Shenandoah Valley from Pennsylvania to Virginia had a rich pottery tradition dating from 1750 and was still producing in the early twentieth century. Hagerstown, where a number of potters trained in the German tradition settled after 1750, was one of the early Valley pottery-producing centers. This slip-decorated, lead-glazed earthenware mixing bowl marked "P. Bell," with its cream and dark brown wavy lines on a tan base, has the Germanic flavor characteristic of the early ceramics of Hagerstown.

Peter Bell, born in 1775, was the son of a Captain Peter Bell who emigrated from Weisbaden, Germany, to Hagerstown in 1765. It is not known to whom the younger Bell was apprenticed, although the style of his work suggests the Weis family of potters, among the earliest working in Hagerstown. By 1800 Bell was in partnership, and in 1805 he was running his own pottery. In the 1820s he moved to Winchester, but he later returned to Hagerstown, where he died in 1847. Three of his sons, and many more of his grandsons, also were potters.

Gift of Mr. Titus Geesey, acc. 2352-1.   *FA*

24,
25,
26,
27,
28,
29

Six pieces of earthenware. Stoneware, an important export commodity of the middle and upper east coast states, was not produced in any quantity in the South until after 1825. Earthenware, however, was made throughout the Backcountry from the mid-eighteenth century on. The trade was dominated by German potters until the end of the century. Major potting districts existed in western Maryland, the northern Shenandoah Valley, and the central piedmont of North Carolina, where the Moravians, in terms of style, technique, and quantity of production, were among the top potters in early America.

The Staffordshire style, which employed Chinese porcelain detailing such as floral sprigs and double-intertwined handles, was brought to the Moravian town of Salem, North Carolina, in the early 1770s, resulting in a significant production of sophisticated English-type pottery there. Apprentices of the potters in Salem left to carry on their own businesses, but relatively few attained the quality of their masters. Phillip Jacob Meyer (1771–1801) was apprenticed to Gottfried Aust (1722–88) and served briefly under Rudolf Christ (1750–1833). By 1793 he had purchased land in Randolph County, about forty miles southeast of Salem, where he operated a pottery until 1799. The "Whieldon"-like underglaze sponging of copper and manganese on the bowl shown here (24, left) is like that used in Salem. The light color of the clay body and the somewhat unrefined form of the piece suggest an attribution to Meyer. *Gift of Mr. and Mrs. George M. Davis, acc. 3553.*

Some of the finest slip-decorated pottery in America was produced by the Moravian masters Aust and Christ. A relatively simple plate (25, below left) with a Guilford County history has "grass"-like flourishes common to pieces from Rudolf Christ's shop, but the wide, flat rim, or "marley," is unlike most Salem plates of the period and may indicate the work of Jacob Meyer. Many such decorated plates show little sign of use, in keeping with their original intent as true "decorative art." *Acc. 2877.*

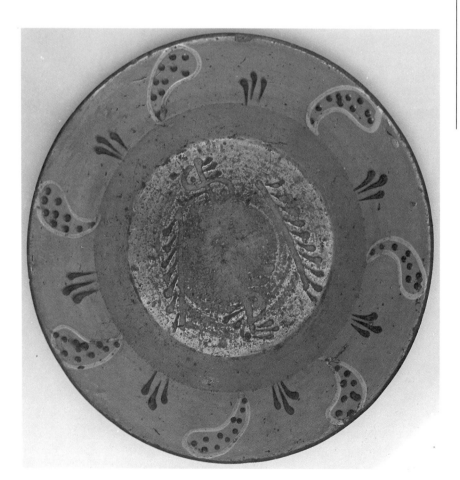

Great elegance of form was not always the domain of decorative wares. A utilitarian storage jar (26, right) of 1800–1840 has the deeply coved neck, globular form, and pronounced rim and foot typical of the wares produced in southwestern Virginia and northeastern Tennessee. The Germanic tradition of this pot is evident in the graceful extruded handles—that is, handles formed through a template under pressure rather than "pulled." Black iron oxide, a byproduct of the blacksmith's forge, was used as the colorant for the lead glaze. *Gift of G. Wilson Douglas, Jr., acc. 3655.*

Without archaeological evidence, it is often impossible to make sound attributions of earthenwares. A fat lamp (27, below) descended in a Randolph County, North Carolina, family with a plate and a jar, all attributable to the same shop. The jar is signed "Henry Watkins." Watkins, a Quaker potter of New Salem, was born in Randolph County in 1799. In 1821 he took "Joseph Wadkins, aged 10½, formerly bound to Seth Hinshaw, as apprentice to the potter's trade." *Acc. 3252-3.*

The green-glazed fish bottle (28, top) is the work of Rudolf Christ, who retired as master of the Salem pottery in 1822. Christ began the production of press-molded figures of many types shortly after 1800, closely following the Staffordshire tradition. An 1819 inventory of the pottery lists four sizes of "fish" at 5*d*., 9*d*., 10*d*., and 1*s*.2*d*.; the example shown here is the smallest of those made by Christ. One pair of plaster press-molds for this bottle still exists. None of the Salem bottles are glazed on the interior, indicating that they were not intended for liquid storage. *Gift of Mr. and Mrs. Ben Willis, acc. 3096.*

A major example of Shenandoah Valley earthenware whimsy is a lion (29, bottom) evidently intended as a doorstop. Made about 1850 for a niece of the Strasburg, Virginia, potter Solomon Bell, the green-eyed lion has a mane of extruded clay strips glazed with manganese. The body is entirely hollow inside, for a solid figure would have cracked while drying or firing. The body was formed from a thrown cylinder, and the head and legs were sculpted. Solomon Bell (1817–82) was born in Hagerstown, the son of the potter Peter Bell (23), with whom he worked until 1839. After working in his brother John Bell's Waynesboro, Pennsylvania, shop, Bell established his own pottery in Strasburg, located in Shenandoah County. A prolific artisan, Bell produced both earthenware and stoneware. *Acc. 2024-95.* JB

30

Gorget, by Thomas W. Machen, New Bern, 1800–1825. Although not a Backcountry product, this silver gorget was made for a western piedmont patron, an Indian named Finey George, probably a member of the Creek tribe. Gorgets, a symbolic remnant of the neckpiece of medieval armor, were worn until the late eighteenth century by commissioned officers of various armies, including Americans. Perhaps because gorgets indicated high rank, Indians were particularly fond of them; portraits of warriors and chiefs in full regalia by artists such as Charles Bird King document the use of gorgets by various tribes well into the nineteenth century. Machen was working in New Bern at least by 1800, when he announced a move from "Craven-street into Middle-street." The restrained Neoclassical wriggle-work border with which he ornamented the gorget evidently did not satisfy Finey George, who used the back of the piece to practice his own engraving skills and then added the two millipede-like devices crawling from the corners. *Acc. 2544.*

JB

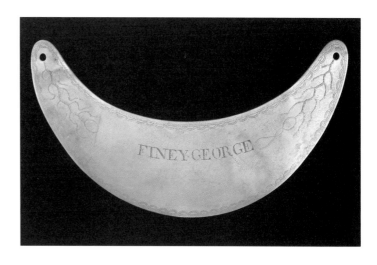

31

Fireback, by the Aera Furnace, York County, South Carolina, 1778–80. Although the merchant furnaces of the Shenandoah Valley dominated the iron trade, the ore beds of the western piedmont of North and South Carolina sustained a lesser iron industry there. By 1779 William Hill and Isaac Hayne, whose initials are on this fireback, had completed the construction of the Aera Furnace near the Catawba River, the first works erected in South Carolina. Established in wartime, it produced not only household goods but "Swivel Guns and Cahorns [cohorns, or small mortars], of any size, 2, 3, or 4 Pounders, with Balls to suit." The "LIBERTY OR DEATH" slogan on the fireback proved to be an omen; the British destroyed the furnace in June 1780, and the following year Hayne was hanged in Charleston. Hill, the actual proprietor, did not put the furnace into blast again until 1786.

Purchased with funds provided by the Seth Sprague Educational and Charitable Foundation, acc. 3119.

JB

32 Pair of andirons, northern Shenandoah Valley of Virginia, 1800–1820. After the Revolution, several furnaces in the Valley produced figural andirons, all of which are "open" castings run on the furnace floor, and at least six different patterns of Valley andirons with heads or busts have been recorded. The 1795 inventory of Isaac Zane's Marlboro Furnace even lists a pattern for "Dog Irons." A large variety of andirons with simple cabriole legs and architectural pedestals seem to have been made in Page and Shenandoah counties; one probable source was the Redwell Furnace near Luray, which operated under various names until at least 1840.

That the Shenandoah furnaces exported quantities of cast iron is evident in the history of these andirons, which were found in the Tidewater near Tappahannock, Virginia. Similar andirons with scattered coastal Virginia and North Carolina histories are known. *Acc. 2547.*   *JB*

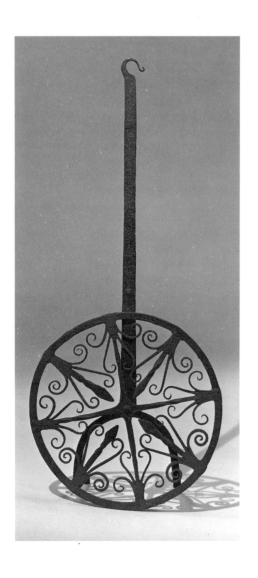

33 Wrought-iron revolving trivet, Kentucky, late eighteenth century. The design of this trivet is much like that of seventeenth-century American, British, and French examples. Its handle is divided into a two-part prong that forms two of the three feet that support it; the other foot is applied halfway down the handle. A spinning circular platform made up of several fleur-de-lis designs is applied at the center of the prong with an iron pentil. Trivets of this type were placed in the coals of a fire; the revolving tops allowed for even cooking.

Gift of Robert B. Hicks III, acc. 3989.   *FA*

34, 35, 36 Three longrifles. The importance of the flintlock longrifle to Backcountry settlers is evident in familiar phrases such as "lock, stock, and barrel" or "only a flash in the pan." The "rifle gun," as it often was called in early records, was a German development of the late fifteenth century. It was discovered that spiraled grooves cut in the bore of a weapon provided considerably more accuracy to a linen-patched lead ball than a smooth bore. This discovery may have derived from the ancient practice of mounting the fletching (feathers) of an arrow at a slight angle to provide a stabilizing in-flight spin to the shaft.

By the end of the seventeenth century, the Germanic sporting rifle was a highly developed firearm. Most rifles were short-barreled so that they could be slung at the hunter's back during the chase, for most hunting of large game was carried out on horseback. However, *büchsen für die pirsch*, or "stalking rifles," with long barrels were also used on the Continent, their greater sight radius providing accuracy at long ranges. It was these rifles that provided the tradition of the American longrifle, which was introduced in the German settlements of Pennsylvania and had spread into the upper South by the mid-eighteenth century. American gunmakers developed a national style from the basic German design, elaborating on the construction and ornamentation of the "box," as it was called, in the

rifle's buttstock. This "patchbox," as it is known today, housed cleaning implements, greased linen patches, or simply grease. Owing to a phrase in a War of 1812 ballad that referred to Andrew Jackson's deadly Kentucky riflemen, the term "Kentucky" rifle became popular at some point during the nineteenth century, even though that state was not known as a gunmaking center.

Few American arts demonstrate a stronger development of regional style than gunmaking. In the South, the German settlements of western Maryland and the Shenandoah Valley of Virginia contained the largest numbers of gunsmiths. Following their European heritage, southern longrifles of the pre-Revolutionary period tend to have ample buttstock proportions, with buttplates that have relatively little curve and widths approaching or exceeding two inches. Although of a later period, 1795–1800, the longrifle (34, below) from the Wythe-Pulaski county area of southwestern Virginia shows much of the architectural fullness characteristic of earlier pieces. Stocked in maple, which is typical of American rifles, the rifle has iron furniture. Iron mounts, preferred in the southern Appalachian region, were more expensive to produce than the cast-brass mounts more commonly found elsewhere. The incised carving on this rifle relates the piece to work produced in Winchester, Virginia's most important riflemaking center. *Acc. 2433.*

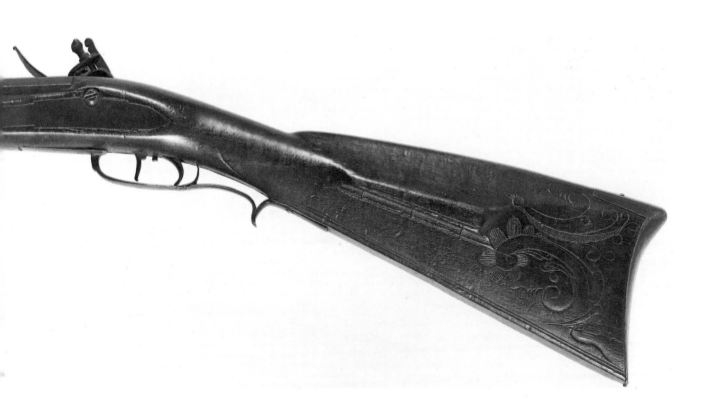

North Carolina's gunmaking centers were located in the piedmont from Guilford County west to the Catawba Valley. One of the most artistic schools of gunsmithing centered in the German settlements of southeastern Rowan County. Born in this area in 1813, the gunsmith John Eagle proudly signed the patchbox lid of a longrifle (35, top) and inscribed one silver inlay with the surprisingly late date "January 14th, 1836." This brass-mounted rifle, with its profuse inlay and elaborate relief carving, is more typical of southern rifles of the 1810–20 period; here the earlier style reveals the conservative preference of Germanic artisans and their patrons. This rifle represents the fully developed American form in its slender stock and elaborate patchbox. Characteristic of the Rowan school is the sharply coved cheekpiece, the exceptional length of the patchbox, and the vestigial "daisy" pattern of the upper portion of the patchbox head. *Donated by Gordon Gray, Jr., Burton C. Gray, Boyden Gray, and Bernard Gray in memory of Jane Craig Gray, acc. 3479-1.*

Also revealing an exceptionally strong regional style is an 1815–25 longrifle (36, bottom) attributed to Patrick Hoy of Spartanburg County, South Carolina, on the basis of other examples signed by Hoy. Because of the southward movement of gunmakers, the influence of the major Pennsylvania gunmaking center, Lancaster, remained strong in some details. Here the classic Lancaster "daisy" pattern of patchbox finial occurs in an attenuated form, yet one more recognizable than the same motif on the John Eagle rifle. There is no reason to believe, however, that Hoy ever worked in Pennsylvania. Born in Ireland about 1786, he died in Spartanburg County in 1860, his inventory including such things as "1 Lot of Gun Barrels." Hoy's "Gun Smith Tools" were worth $15, but his "growing Crop" was valued at $265, indicating that Hoy, like many rural tradesmen, was a farmer-artisan. A very unusual feature of this rifle, and one shared by other upper piedmont South Carolina longrifles, is the use of a two-piece bone buttplate accompanied by bone inset at the toe of the buttstock. This follows an ancient European heritage; many fine crossbows and wheel-lock arms of the sixteenth century were extensively decorated with bone. In this instance, the use of bone would have been more expensive than a brass casting. *Acc. 3957.* JB

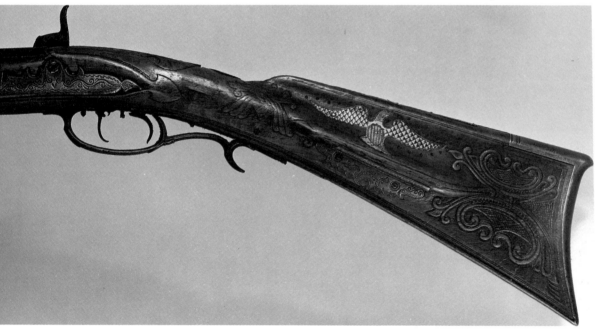

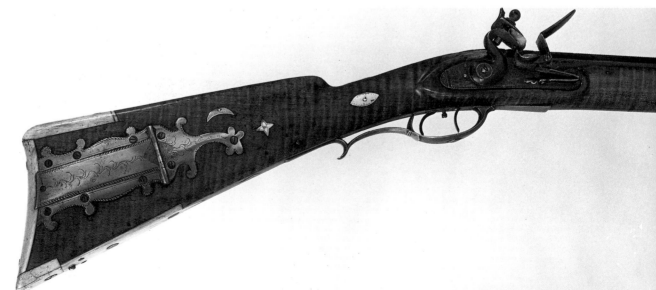

37

Dressing table, Orange County, North Carolina, 1765–80. Furniture of the eastern piedmont of North Carolina frequently shows the influence of coastal styles owing to the westward migration of tradesmen. One of a sizable number of tables and chairs from the same shop, which was probably located in Hillsborough, this walnut dressing table mixes several styles. The strongly projecting profile of the claw feet relates the work of this cabinet-maker to styles prevalent in Williamsburg, and the baluster turnings of the upper legs resemble turnings from Surry and Sussex counties south of the James River. A third Virginia detail is the lack of a rail above the drawer. This table descended in the Webb family of Hillsborough; many of the other pieces descended from Richard Bennehan (1743–1825) of Stagville plantation, about twenty miles east of Hillsborough. Bennehan, a native of Virginia who moved to North Carolina in 1768, owned over 4,000 acres by 1800.

Gift of Mr. Joseph B. Cheshire, acc. 3777-2.   JB

38

Cabinet, central piedmont North Carolina, 1780–90. This unusual cabinet evidently was used for the storage of valuables rather than spices, for no trace of the latter remains in the interior drawers. The profile of the ogee feet, the heavy lunetted banding outlining the door, and the drawer construction relate the piece to a large group of furniture attributed to an anonymous shop probably located in the lower Yadkin River valley near Rowan County. A Backcountry approach to construction is evident in the feet and bed molding, both cut from single pieces of board. The fluted consoles under the projecting cornice piers are a formal detail that contrasts with the bold inlaid fylfot ornamenting the door head.

Gift of Mr. and Mrs. Philip Hanes, acc. 1071-1.   JB

39

Hanging shelf, western piedmont North Carolina, 1800–1810. The early cut nails in this piece provide a date range that is later than its style. It is made of cherry, yellow pine, and poplar. The heavy stringing of its shaped fascia and the drawer front seem to relate the shelf to the previous cabinet, but this piece shows less refinement in both inlay and construction—the backboards, for example, are exposed at the sides—and is considerably more Germanic in style. It is attributed to the Catawba River valley region, consisting of Iredell, Catawba, Lincoln, and Gaston counties. The shaping of its sides makes them a miniature version of those of a kitchen cupboard. The tuliplike inlay of the top resembles painted decoration.

Gift of Mr. and Mrs. Ralph P. Hanes, acc. 256-4.

JB

Linen press, attributed to James Gheen, Rowan County, 1780–1800. This walnut, poplar, and yellow pine linen press, along with nineteen other case pieces, is attributed to James Gheen on the strength of a 1794 bill found in one of the pieces, which lists a desk and bookcase at £15.12.6 supplied by Gheen and credits Reverend Samuel Mc-Corkle, a Presbyterian minister in Rowan County, with £5.15.0. This linen press has many construction characteristics considered typical of Gheen's work, including a single heavy glue block that thins at the center and traverses each side of the case from front to rear. Other Gheen characteristics are the vertical pitch of the cornice cove, the fluted case chamfers, the narrow bevels of the raised panels, and the heavy ogee feet.

Gheen probably immigrated to North Carolina from Pennsylvania; by 1778 he had settled in Rowan County. He purchased several tracts of land in that area, as well as property in Salisbury. Gheen died in 1796; his grandson Warren Gheen was a cabinetmaker in Salisbury. *Acc. 2024-51.* *FA*

41

Corner cupboard, Orange or Alamance County, North Carolina, 1775–85. Corner cupboards are one of the most frequently encountered furniture forms in piedmont North Carolina. Although the MESDA example has no history, a virtually identical cupboard, also of walnut, with a history of descent in the Johnston family of Orange County provides a regional attribution for this example. Typical of Backcountry furniture was the cabinetmaker's or joiner's "making do" with the hardware available. In this instance, two sizes of table hinges were flush-inset on the stiles of the cupboard to suspend the doors, and a small thumb latch, very likely a local product, was used to secure the upper doors. The bracket feet do not return along the front of the case, lending a very real sense of instability to the cupboard.

This cupboard is made in two pieces, a form of construction often associated with German artisans. An even stronger German feature is the fact that the backboards are dovetailed to the tops and bottoms of both sections, a characteristic not observed on southern Backcountry cupboards in the British tradition. These features suggest a possible connection with the German settlement of eastern Alamance County. The inclusion of a dentil course carved into the ogee upper element of the cornice reveals the hand of a rural-trained artisan. *Acc. 1004-1.*   *JB*

42 Press, central piedmont North Carolina, 1770–90. Made in southeastern Randolph County or neighboring southwestern Chatham County, this press is one of a number of pieces by the same artisan, known as the "peaked apron" cabinetmaker from the distinctive shaping of the bases of his work. The wood is entirely yellow pine; the red paint of the carcass and doors is set off with accents of white and black. Also typical of this artisan's work are the extensive edging of the case with an ogee mold-ing and the use of a series of sawn lunettes under the cornice in place of the more normal dentils. The arched heads of the upper doors, the massive bracket feet, the flush-fitted drawers, the use of pintle hinges, and the shallower depth of the upper portion, which provides a "step" over the drawers, all reveal a basic German format.

Gift of the estate of Katherine Hanes, acc. 2073-22.

JB

43 Desk and bookcase, central piedmont North Carolina, 1780–1800. The area of the North Carolina piedmont between Alamance and Mecklenburg counties is known for the extensive production of case furniture—largely chests of drawers—perched on low, squared cabriole legs. Most such pieces do not have bases constructed as separate frames, but this desk and bookcase, probably made in southern Guilford County or northern Randolph County, is an exception. It represents perhaps the earliest known example of this cabinetmaking tradition in the region. The most imposing feature of this desk and bookcase is the peculiar Gothic-like pediment, which was made as a separate unit. The legs are remarkably like the squat cabriole legs of fifteenth-century Chinese tables. In addition to the highly vernacular pediment, the massive construction of the piece—thick carcass sides, corbeled interior partitions, and drawer frames—indicates a cabinetmaker with a rural background. The drawer bottoms are fastened to the backs with wooden pins rather than nails, a detail generally associated with, but not confined to, the German cabinetmaking tradition.

Gift of Mr. and Mrs. James Douglas, acc. 3541. JB

Desk and bookcase, Frederick, Maryland, 1780–90. This walnut and poplar desk and bookcase has a long Frederick history. Its interior is fitted with a carved prospect and shaped drawers and letter compartments; ten secret drawers have been fitted behind the prospect. An unusual feature of the desk is its quarter columns; these, including the upper and lower blocks, are formed from single pieces of walnut rather than the usual three parts and are turned with capitals that are part of the fluted members. Straight frieze-pedimented pieces similar to this example were being made in Philadelphia shortly before the Revolution, and they probably began appearing in outer Pennsylvania and southward in the 1780s. *Acc. 3985.* FA

45

Desk and bookcase, by John Shearer, Martinsburg, West Virginia, 1801–6. John Shearer's shop in Martinsburg, which at the time was part of Frederick County, Virginia, is known for the production of carefully made but often bizarre furniture. Desks, desks and bookcases, chests of drawers, tables of various types, a tall clock, and a cellaret from his shop have been recorded. Shearer's history is elusive. He appears to have been born in Scotland about 1765, and he died in Washington County, Maryland, in 1810. An inscription in the desk portion of the desk and bookcase, "made by me, John Shearer Septr. 1801 from Edinburgh 1775/ Made in Martinsburgh," apparently documents Shearer's origins. He was somewhat fanatic with inscriptions. The desk and bookcase is signed twenty times, and the bookcase is dated 1806, indicating that the piece was a "marriage" by the cabinetmaker himself. Another message scrawled inside the desk yields Shearer's political sentiments: "God Save the King." Similar phrases appear in other Shearer pieces, including "From a Tory."

Shearer's style is an eclectic blend of Baroque, Rococo, and Neoclassical with a heavy emphasis on architectural detail, as both the bookcase cornice and the desk interior reveal. These features, combined with a naive interpretation of designs such as the feet, relate to Scottish cabinetmaking trends of the late eighteenth century, suggesting that Shearer very well may have been apprenticed to another Scots cabinetmaker working in Virginia. His use of woods is just as diverse as his mixed styles. The desk carcass is of walnut, but the drawer fronts, the baize-lined fallboard, and portions of the interior are cherry. The bookcase also is cherry, but its finials and pediment volute bosses are mulberry. Yellow pine, walnut, and oak were used as secondary woods, the oak for drawer frames. Typical of this eccentric cabinetmaker's work is the diagonal and vertical installation of the drawer pulls. *Acc. 2979.*

JB

46 Desk and bookcase, central piedmont North Carolina, 1790–1800. This massive cherry piece shows strong regional influence as well as the influence of outside styles. The unusual pediment and squarish proportions are reminiscent of both German and Dutch Baroque furniture, but the arrangement of the interior of the desk and the use of slender quarter columns are in the Delaware Valley tradition. The rural translation of urban styles is revealed in various details, however. For example, both the bases and the capitals of the columns are the same turning, and the upper rails of the bookcase doors are ponderously wide. The use of small drawers as fallboard supports was favored in the counties west of Philadelphia. The exaggerated responds of the ogee feet are typical of furniture from the eastern Catawba Valley area. Another desk and bookcase from the same shop, also with an Iredell County history, is made entirely in the Neoclassical style. *Acc. 2015.* *JB*

47 Chest on frame, attributed to Jesse Needham, Randolph County, North Carolina, 1790–1800. The original die-struck brasses on this chest of drawers belie the early style of the piece, which has frame shaping and a foot form that might be expected of a Philadelphia piece of the 1740s. This chest is highly characteristic of a large group of furniture consisting of at least twenty-five pieces, all attributed to Jesse Needham, who was born about 1776 and moved to Ohio in 1839. A native of Pasquotank County in the northeastern portion of the state, Needham must have served his apprenticeship after moving to Randolph County in 1792, for the Pennsylvania influence in his work is not reflected in furniture of the North Carolina Albemarle. Needham's other case furniture, particularly desks, makes a strong Philadelphia statement with serpentine-shaped interior drawers, slim quarter columns, well-detailed moldings, and graceful ogee feet with spurred responds. The attribution of this chest to Needham is based on inscriptions scrawled inside a chest on frame made for one of Needham's cousins. Virtually all of the group is walnut with poplar secondary.

Gift of Mr. and Mrs. J. G. Johnson, acc. 3027.   *JB*

48 Desk and bookcase, by Peter Eddleman, Lincoln County, North Carolina, 1799. Peter Eddleman or Adelmann (1762–1847) was born in Bucks County, Pennsylvania, and moved with his parents to Rowan County, North Carolina, in 1768. By 1791 he was operating his own shop in Lincoln County. In 1799 he made this cherry desk and bookcase for a neighboring planter, Thomas Rhyne, whose two-story brick house of that year still stands in northern Gaston County. Seven pieces of furniture have been attributed to Eddleman, including a large and highly ornamented china press also made for Rhyne. That Eddleman must have been apprenticed to a former Pennsylvania artisan may be seen in the Delaware Valley–style shaping of the drawers of the desk's interior, but the wide, fluted prospect door diverges from urban work, as does the lack of a bed mold under the interior. Also breaking with the Philadelphia tradition are the lower quarter columns, which have inlaid "fluting." Eddleman's rural style is evident in the utilization of base turnings for the capitals of the columns and in the wide stiles of the rather low bookcase, all contrasting with the formal nature of the Doric dentil of the crown molding. *Acc. 2564-2.*   *JB*

49 Pembroke table, by Peter Eddleman, Lincoln County, 1800–1820. The naive blending of vernacular details with urban style can yield a charming composition, as this large walnut Pembroke table demonstrates. The stringing and banded "cuffs" ornamenting the legs of this table break with formality with the return of the inner stringing across the skirts, providing a base for the dramatic lunetted fans. The rural cabinetmaker's lack of knowledge in the specialized technology of Neoclassical inlay is quite apparent in the bands of lozenges and stringing outlining the top and skirt fans. This inlay actually is not banding at all, but over 250 individual lozenges individually inlet into the wood! Eddleman used the same inlay on several case pieces.

Gift of the estate of Katherine Hanes, acc. 2073-26.

JB

China press, attributed to John Swisegood, David-son County, North Carolina, 1820–25. The northeastern corner of Davidson County, the site of a large German settlement, saw the development of a small but significant school of cabinetmaking along Abbots Creek in the early nineteenth century. Mordica Collins (1785–1864), John Swisegood (1796–1874), Jesse Clodfelter (b. 1804), and Jonathan Long (1803–58) were the four artisans responsible for the production of a sizable group of elegantly restrained Neoclassical furniture. Swisegood was the apprentice of Collins; Long and probably Clodfelter were apprentices of Swisegood. The bulk of this group of furniture, which consists of cupboards, presses, desks, chests, and chests of drawers, is in the British tradition; however, the walnut china press illustrated here is a form familiar to the German settlements of southeastern Pennsylvania. The glazed press over a cabinet with drawers and doors seems a derivation of the earlier kitchen cupboard. Although such presses were made in Pennsylvania in large numbers, they are not common in the Carolina Backcountry. Details typical of John Swisegood and other members of the school are the bold coved cornice, the herringbone inlay ornamenting the upper case and central drawer, the commalike inlays on the drawers, and the lunetted flat panels of the cabinet doors. Swisegood moved to McDonough County, Illinois, in 1848, following a familiar pattern of outward migration from the Carolina piedmont at the time. *Acc. 2127.*   *JB*

51 Fireback, by the Vesuvius Furnace, Lincoln County, 1792–1810. The simplicity of this astragal-shaped fireback is typical of the cast iron produced in the Carolina Backcountry. The Vesuvius Furnace was constructed on Anderson Creek in eastern Lincoln County, not far from the Catawba River, and continued to operate into the nineteenth century, producing household wares of various types as well as 30,000 pounds of shot and shells for the United States Government during the War of 1812. The face of the fireback is cast with the legend "VE-SUVIUS FURNACE/ J. GRAHAM." Joseph Graham (52) was the proprietor of the works; he was in partnership with others in the firm of Joseph Graham and Company. *Acc. 2564-1.* JB

52 *Joseph Graham*, miniature, Lincoln County, 1790–1800. The Reinhardt, Forney, Brevard, Davidson, and Graham families dominated the iron industry of the Catawba Valley. Graham (1759–1836), a native of Chester County, Pennsylvania, served as a dragoon in Revolutionary campaigns throughout the western Carolina piedmont, rising to the rank of major. Sometime after the War Graham formed a partnership with John Davidson and Alexander Brevard to produce cast iron. First known as the Iron Company and later as Joseph Graham and Company, the firm had assets valued at over $28,000 in 1804. All three men were planters, engaging in the operation of a furnace, Vesuvius, as a secondary venture. Graham's frame dwelling, located near the furnace site, still stands. He also owned property near Denver and Beatties Ford, also in Lincoln County. The artist who executed this miniature is unknown. *Acc. 2825.* JB

Secretary with bookcase, lower Catawba Valley, North Carolina, 1790–1800. With a history of descent from William Alexander Graham, governor of North Carolina from 1845 to 1849, it is probable that this cherry secretary with bookcase originally was the property of Vesuvius Furnace proprietor Joseph Graham (51, 52), the governor's father. The piece belongs to a group of furniture associated with anonymous cabinetmakers working in southeastern Gaston County or northwestern Mecklenburg County. Joseph Graham's business affairs in Mecklenburg were extensive, and he served as sheriff of that county in the mid-1780s.

Typical of this school of cabinetmaking is the architectural composition of the bookcase, which is in the form of a classical Venetian window complete with fluted pilasters and inlaid arch imposts, a style very popular in southeastern Pennsylvania furniture of the period. The triple-string inlay of the drawer fronts, composed of a pair of opposing compass-drawn arcs with a sprig inlay in the center, is repeated on the hinged front of the secretary and on other work of the same shop and region. Corner cupboards in this group have dovetailed joinery of the tops and backboards, indicating that at least one of the cabinetmakers in this school was of German descent or training.

Gift of Mr. and Mrs. Frank Borden Hanes, acc. 2845.
JB

54

Corner cupboard, attributed to Mordica Collins, Davidson County, 1810–15. Here an arched-head Venetian door—a "Palladian" door in popular terminology—is modified by the use of unusual curved muntins, which with its cusped center light makes for a Gothic interpretation of the classical style. Details of construction date this cupboard among the earliest products of the Davidson County school, to which the furniture attributed to John Swisegood (50) belongs, thereby providing an attribution to Collins, who was Swisegood's master. Swisegood and his apprentices used many of Collins's stylistic details, including the applied "pilasters" with panels and gadrooned heads that have a "sheaf of wheat" appearance. The cable, or rope-carved, stile moldings, carved finials and pediment rosettes, and lunetted cabinet door panels all are hallmarks of the school.

Gift of Mr. and Mrs. James Douglas, acc. 3576.   *JB*

55 Corner cupboard, northern Shenandoah Valley of Virginia, 1790–1810. The arched muntins of this cupboard's Venetian door heads follow a more standard architectural application than the Collins cupboard (54), but here the arch head is compressed and the muntins follow converging arcs in a naive fashion. The walnut cupboard is covered with detail, much of which is typical of pieces with histories that converge on the area of Shenandoah and Rockingham counties in the Valley. Most unusual is the use of applied light hardwood features such as the handles and finials of the urns atop the pilasters. The C-scrolled spandrels in the upper lights of the doors are an uncommon detail as well. The finials and rosettes are painted red. The commodious width of the cupboard, the inclusion of the inlaid initials of the owner, and the wooden pins used to attach the moldings and pilaster all attest to the essentially German population of this region of the Valley.

William L. Gray Purchase Fund, acc. 3564. JB

56 Tall clock, by John Fessler, Frederick, Maryland, 1785–1800. In the southern Backcountry, the clock-making trade received the greatest encouragement in the German communities, where the efficient use of time was a major concern. Western Maryland is known for its large production of clocks, and a particularly prolific clockmaker was John Fessler of Frederick. When Fessler died in 1820, his obituary described him as a "resident of this place upwards of forty years" and called his death a "serious loss to the community." Fessler was working in Frederick at least as early as 1784, when he took an apprentice to "the art and Trade of a Clock maker." Although many silversmiths advertised themselves as watch and clock makers, it is interesting to observe that very few of them actually did more than repair work. Southern tradesmen capable of making clock movements largely specialized in that work, frequently also producing other metal instruments such as surveyors' compasses.

The cases of Fessler's clocks vary in style. In sixteen Fessler clocks recorded by MESDA, the work of at least six cabinetmakers is evident; the shop that produced the walnut case of this eight-day clock (right) also produced three others. The basic Philadelphia format common to clock cases in the southern counties of Pennsylvania and into Maryland and southward is evident in the style of the carved flame finials, the rosettes, the dramatic sweep of the scrolled pediment, and various other architectural elements of the cove, waist, and plinth. *Acc. 2024-41.* JB

57 Tall clock, Chester, South Carolina, 1810–20. The white dial of this eight-day clock (far right) is signed "Jno. McKee/ Chester/ S:C," and a label is pasted inside the waist door giving notice that "all kinds of Clocks, with, or without cases" were offered at "J. McKee's Clock Factory, Chester Court House." Despite all this apparent documentation, however, only the cherry case of this clock was made in South Carolina. Many tradesmen who advertised themselves as clockmakers relied entirely on movements imported from England, primarily Birmingham, some of them with dials already signed with the American vendor's name. The works of this example are signed by the clockmaker James Hawthorn of Newcastle upon Tyne, England. McKee was a native of County Down, Ireland. There is no documentation of his having actually made clock movements; he was probably just a merchant. Two other clock cases and a corner cupboard have been attributed to the same anonymous cabinetmaker that produced this case for McKee or one of his patrons. *Acc. 2024-140.* JB

58 *John Jameson, Sr.*, oil on poplar, by Francis? Cezeron, Culpeper County, Virginia, 1809. Very little is known about Cezeron. He was a dancing and French instructor in Lancaster, Pennsylvania, in 1806, and from 1810 to 1811 he advertised as "Cezeron," portraitist, in Frederick, Maryland, and Fredericksburg, Virginia. Records indicate that he had returned to Lancaster by 1811 or 1812. Apparently he mainly painted profiles, generally described as crude, in the manner of other French artists like Saint-Mémin. This painting is inscribed on the reverse "John Jameson, Sen./ aged 59 years/ Painted by Cicerong/ June 1809/ 1809," apparently not by the artist, for the spelling of his name is anglicized and Jameson's age is not correct.

John Jameson, Sr., was born in 1751. He served on George Washington's staff during the Revolution, was made a colonel, and died in 1810. *Acc. 3229-1.* *FA*

59

Mrs. Peter Lauck, oil on canvas, by Jacob Frymire, Winchester, Virginia, 1801. Jacob Frymire was born in Lancaster, Pennsylvania, between 1765 and 1774. His paintings indicate that he had some type of professional training. From 1799 to 1805 Frymire traveled in Virginia, taking commissions in Winchester, Alexandria, and Warrenton for paintings and miniatures, and by 1806 he was working in Kentucky. He returned to Pennsylvania in 1807 and died on his father's farm in 1822.

Frymire's painting techniques developed subtly through the years that he was itinerant. Although his paintings are characterized by the stiffness and sharpness commonly found in the work of Back-country artists, Frymire showed some sophistication in solving artistic problems due to a lack of formal training. This portrait of Mrs. Peter Lauck, signed and dated by the artist, is the first recorded Frymire painting that uses a detailed background to enhance the subject's attractiveness.

Amelia Heiskell Lauck was the wife of Peter Lauck, who built the Red Lion Inn in Winchester in 1783. The Laucks operated the inn intermittently until the 1830s. *Acc. 3406.*   *FA*

60

Painted banner, Virginia, 1799. This silk banner is decorated with a painted eagle, "Liberty or Death," "New Market Infantry," nineteen gold stars, and a medallion inscribed "7th Brig./ 13th Regt./ 1799." It is one of only a few eighteenth-century American military flags that have survived. Several entries in the *Calendar of Virginia State Papers* indicate that the 13th Regiment of Militia was formed in Shenandoah County in 1794 as part of the 7th Brigade, 3rd Division; New Market is in that county. A bill dated 8 November 1787 among the executive papers of the Shenandoah County militia contained the following entry for a related banner: "Sept. 12 To Wm. Bushby for painting lettering with gold & shading the Colours of Shennando Militia Making the Colours & sewing silk [£]4.5.0½." *Acc. 2049.*

FA

61 *George Washington*, oil on canvas, by Frederick Kemmelmeyer, Baltimore, or western Maryland, or Virginia, 1795–1805. Ironically enough, likenesses of George Washington in portraiture, fabrics, and ceramics abound all over the Northeast, but are rare in the South. This sensitively drawn if rather naive portrait of Washington was painted by the itinerant artist Frederick Kemmelmeyer; it is one of a number of Washington portraits executed by the artist.

Kemmelmeyer emigrated from Europe to Maryland in 1788. In a Baltimore advertisement of that year, the artist announced his "Drawing-School" and offered to paint "Miniatures and other sizes, in oil and water colors, and Sign Painting upon moderate terms." He remained in Baltimore until 1803, when he moved to Alexandria. By 1805 he was in western Maryland, advertising in Frederick and

Hagerstown newspapers, and records of his presence in Winchester, Virginia, and Shepherdstown (now West Virginia) have been found. He apparently settled in the northern Shenandoah Valley areas of Maryland and Virginia, since the last record of him consists of an 1816 advertisement for his drawing school.

The style and even the format of many of Kemmelmeyer's paintings tend to reflect his notice about sign painting. Most are didactic and lack dimension, many have painted legends at the bottom, and some, like this example, use gilt to highlight details of dress. Kemmelmeyer painted at least two other cameo-format portraits of Washington. The other two show the General with a happier visage, but all three, interestingly, show his smallpox scars—a detail omitted in the more flattering portraits by far more eminent painters. *Acc. 3814.*

JB

62 *The Bloody Sentence of the Jews Against Jesus Christ the Lord and Saviour of the World*, oil on canvas, by Frederick Kemmelmeyer, Baltimore, 1788–1802. This painting, inscribed "Baltimore/ Painted by F. Kemmelmeyer," was based on an as yet unidentified print source. The subject combines all the stages of Jesus's trial by the Jewish judges and Pontius Pilate, incorporates his appearance before both Caiaphas and Pilate, and depicts his robing and crowning with the wreath of thorns. A paper legend at the bottom of the painting consists of a direct transcription of a document entitled "The Sentence of Pontius Pilate," followed by a description of Jesus taken from an Italian apocryphal epistle.

A revival of paintings based on classical, historical, and religious themes in the Italian manner was largely undertaken by Benjamin West and his school as early as 1770, and a few other American artists tried their hands at the religious genre. This example is one of four southern religious paintings dating before 1820 that have been recorded. The others are Gustavus Hesselius's *The Last Supper* (c. 1750), William Joseph Williams's crucifixion scene (c. 1810), and Thomas Coram's *Christ Blessing the Little Children* (c. 1805). *Acc. 3967.* FA

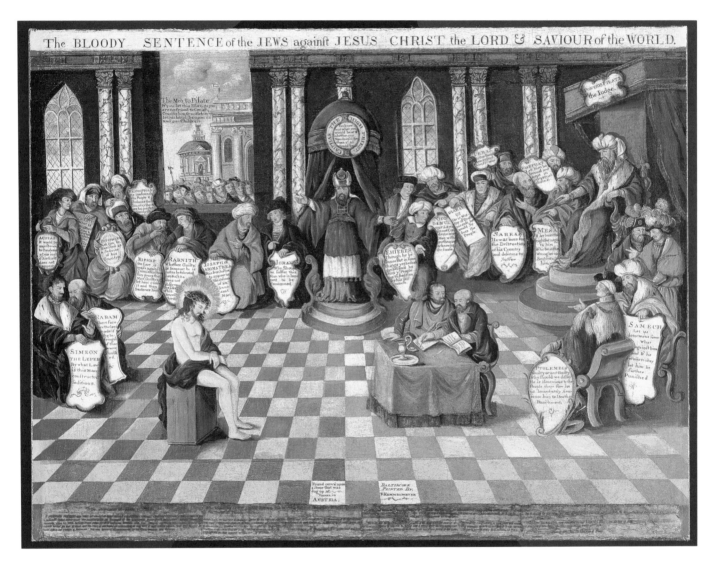

63, 64 *Junction of the Potomac and Shenandoah, Virginia*, watercolor on paper and aquatint, 1808. The watercolor (63, next page, top) of this view was executed in Virginia from an artist's study by William Roberts also in the MESDA collection. The aquatint (64, next page, bottom) is inscribed "Drawn by W. Roberts Esq. Engraved by J. Jeakes" and was published in London, possibly by Conalgi and Company. The arsenal at Harper's Ferry, located in the foreground of these examples, was a popular subject for landscape painters working in western Virginia and Maryland. William Roberts painted several other Virginia landscapes as well, including the

Natural Bridge and the Potomac River, and two of his oils were owned by Thomas Jefferson. In a letter to Jefferson in 1803 Roberts wrote that he was "lately from Norfolk," but was on an excursion to London with his sister. Several histories of his daughter and her husband, as well as inscriptions on two aquatints, including the print in the MESDA collection, indicate that he settled in London at 91 Gloucester Place in Portman Square. Nothing else is known about him.

Douglas Battery and G. Wilson Douglas Purchase Funds, acc. 3424-2 & 3. FA

Sideboard, Winchester area, Virginia, 1795–1805.
Serpentine sideboards were being advertised in the
Valley of Virginia as early as 1799. On 9 October
of that year, Shepherdstown cabinetmaker William
Eaty announced in the *Berkely Intelligencer* that
"gentlemen and ladies may be supplied with the
newest and neatest fashions, such as mahogany
sash, corner, cylinder, and serpentine Sideboards."
Made of mahogany, mahogany veneer, yellow pine,
and walnut, with light wood inlays, this sideboard
combines urban design and veneers with regional
inlays and is an excellent illustration of the sophisticated work produced by some Valley of Virginia
shops. Its unusual serpentine center with ovolo
ends is not common to extant sideboards. However, its shape, design, and inlays are repeated on
another Winchester sideboard, and a third serpentine-shaped example with cavetto ends, the same
dashed inlay, and a similar tulip inlay has a Winchester area history.

Gift of Mrs. Bahnson Gray, acc. 3350.   FA

66 Ten-plate stove, attributed to the Isabella Furnace of Catoctin Works, Frederick County, Maryland, 1815–20. Six- and ten-plate "pipe" stoves, as they were called, were made as early as the 1760s and became popular in Pennsylvania and the South after the Revolution. Long attributed to the Isabella Furnace in Page County, Virginia, this stove instead is probably a product of the Isabella Furnace at the huge Catoctin works in Maryland, which by the early nineteenth century comprised several furnace operations.

One of the later partners in the Catoctin operation was Benjamin Blackford, who leased the works from 1802 until 1812; it was Blackford, along with John Arthur, who bought the Redwell Furnace in Page County, Virginia, in 1808, and renamed it "Isabella." It is because all known Virginia stoves have floor-cast flat plates rather than flask-cut curved plates that this stove is now attributed to Maryland. Yet a third Isabella Furnace was operated on the Potomac River in Maryland by the firm of Brien and McPherson, who in 1806 purchased the Antietam Furnace and renamed it.

The source of the ornament on this stove is clear. Robert Wellford of Philadelphia operated his composition ornament manufactory from at least 1801

until 1820. In 1807 he advertised his "cement of solid and tenacious materials, which when properly incorporated and pressed into moulds, receives a fine relievo." One of the scenes that he intended for the ornamentation of mantel tablets—and that has been found on at least three such tablets—was an elaborate rendition of the 1813 Battle of Lake Erie. Wellford evidently adapted his master pattern for this design from one of the popular engravings of the battle, probably the *Second View of Com. Perry's Victory* painted by Michele-Felice Corné in 1812 and engraved by W. B. Annin of Boston. Wellford offered variations of this composition scene: the one used by the Isabella Furnace for making the stove-casting patterns bears the legend "WE HAVE MET THE ENEMY AND THEY ARE OURS." *Acc. 2498.* *JB*

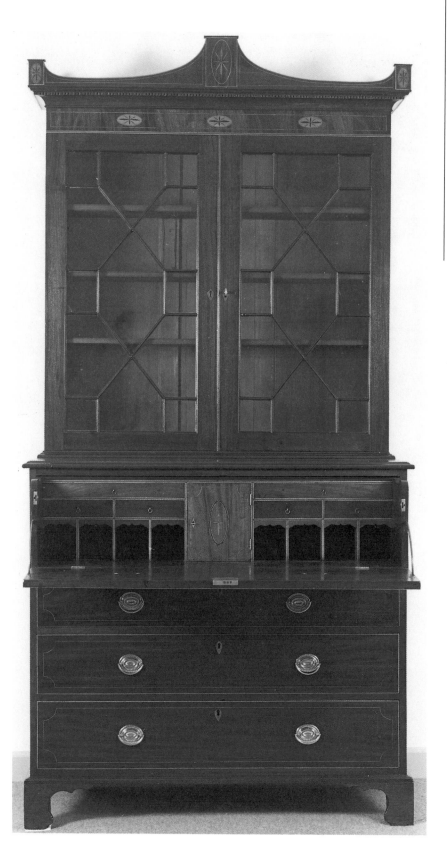

Secretary and bookcase, by William Little, Anson County, North Carolina, 1805–10. This Neoclassical mahogany, poplar, and yellow pine secretary and bookcase with mahogany inlay has the initials "WL" incised in the top of its secretary drawer. It was made by William Little (1775–1848). Two other similar Little secretaries, one of which is signed, have been recorded, but only this example has a molded top base, which dates it about 1805—earlier than the others. Little, who was born in northern England, worked in Norfolk and Charleston before settling in the piedmont North Carolina community of Sneedsboro, where he worked from 1801 to about 1818. His furniture is notable for the purity of its English design and construction in an area where such characteristics usually were mixed with strong German traits. For example, the drawers of this secretary are stopped by blocks at the back case sides, an English construction method. Little also imitated certain Charleston design elements such as straight bracket feet under a molded base and molded tops like the one illustrated here. He used mahogany as a primary wood for much of his furniture; apparently he was the only piedmont North Carolina artisan to do so.

Gift of Mr. and Mrs. James W. Douglas, acc. 3264.

FA

68 Pembroke table, attributed to William Little, Anson County, North Carolina, 1805–10. Made of mahogany, poplar, yellow pine, and oak, with light and dark wood inlays, this table was attributed to William Little on the basis of its construction and the elongated four-petal design in its rectangular panel, a Norfolk detail adopted by Little. Its construction matches that of a tea table, made of cherry, which descended in Little's family, as well as a card table found in the Sneedsboro area. This table's inlay pattern is unique to Little and strongly resembles that of the secretary and bookcase in the MESDA collection (67).

On loan to the museum, acc. 2618. FA

69 Sideboard, attributed to William Little, Anson County, North Carolina, 1802–18. This mahogany and yellow pine Neoclassical sideboard is attributed to William Little on the strength of its construction and its inlay designs, particularly the trifid-top keyhole escutcheons, the stars, and the bellflower pendants on the legs. The inlaid diamond lozenges at the tops of the leg stiles and in the panel of the center drawer are reminiscent of Charleston work. This example is one of only two serpentine-front sideboards attributed to Little; the other is much plainer with only inlaid stringing for decoration.

Acc. 3962. FA

70 Sideboard, Georgia, 1800–1810. This sideboard (above), with its serpentine center, concave ends, and rare combination of birch and walnut as primary woods, has a Warrenton, Georgia, history and may have been made in the Augusta area. Although six-leg sideboards with upper decks were a common Charleston form, the unusual shape and woods of this piece indicate that it was not made in the Low Country, where mahogany was the popular primary wood, and satinwood, holly, and maple were the usual inlay woods. In fact, no other recorded piece of southern furniture uses birch and walnut to achieve a two-tone effect; only in New England was this a common combination. *Acc. 2105.*

FA

71 Sideboard, Spartanburg–Greenville County area of South Carolina, 1795–1805. Three other sideboards and several other pieces have been attributed to the upcountry South Carolina shop that made this walnut and yellow pine sideboard(below); however, several features, including a flush bead outlining the front skirt and brackets and full dust boards, relate the work to that of northeastern North Carolina. Some unusual signatures of this cabinetmaker found on this sideboard are the cockbeading, which is cut in relief rather than applied, the burl-grained panels inserted on the stile and panels of the case, the black-stained pine top, and the gallery rail supported by gold-painted balustrades. *Acc. 3977.*

FA

72　　Coverlet, by Amelia Chenoweth Nash, Kentucky, 1800–1810. This linen and cotton coverlet is decorated with white-on-white embroidery, deflected-element work, and drawnwork and is bound with a woven fringe. For the drawnwork, the threads of the fabric were cut or drawn away, and those remaining were stitched together, creating a netlike pattern. The deflected-element work was produced by pushing aside ground threads and binding or stitching them in clusters to form a motif. The vibrant floral designs of this coverlet, based on patterns dating as early as 1725, demonstrate how earlier designs were incorporated into much later work; this was particularly common in the Backcountry.

Amelia Chenoweth, daughter of Richard and Margaret Chenoweth, married Harmon Nash on 1 June 1792, the day Kentucky became a state. Two similar coverlets, one with a Kentucky history and the other with a Georgia history, have also been recorded. *Acc. 2033-3.*　　　　　　　　　　*FA*

73   Desk and bookcase, by Isaac Evans, Maysville, Kentucky, 1800–1810. This cherry and poplar desk and bookcase is signed on the interior backboards "Made by my hans Isaac Evans, Maysville, K." Its cabinetwork is of the first order. Its chamfered corners were inlaid to resemble fluting, and its interior is decorated with inlay. An unusual construction feature, perhaps a signature of the cabinetmaker, is the bottom dovetail on the interior drawers, which is shaped differently from its counterparts. Although it retains several Rococo details, such as the overlapping drawers, this desk and bookcase also demonstrates Evans's familiarity with Neoclassical designs.

   Isaac Evans probably arrived, via Pennsylvania and Indiana, in Maysville in Mason County sometime after 1797. By 1810 he was living in Montgomery County, and in 1834 he moved to Fleming County. No other examples of his work have been recorded. *Acc. 2043-2.*   *FA*

74   Desk with linen cabinet, central Kentucky, 1795–1810. Kentucky is known for its production of colorful Neoclassical furniture with fanciful inlay and the extensive use of highly figured cherry, the usual primary wood of that state. Walnut is rare in Kentucky furniture, but this desk is of walnut and walnut veneer, all with fiddleback figures. Although the border banding, skirt fan, and floral oval cartouches in the cabinet doors all fit the Kentucky vernacular, the rayed parquetry composition of the door veneers is unique. The doors conceal sliding trays intended for the storage of folded fabrics, much in the fashion of an urban clothespress; the upper portion consists of a writing desk and is unusual only in the support of the fallboard, which is hung on chains. Most Kentucky furniture was produced in Lexington and the surrounding towns and counties, and it is evident that Shenandoah Valley and even Baltimore styles influenced its makers.

   On loan to the museum, acc. 3480.   *JB*

75 Work stand, South Carolina, 1805–10. The bird's-eye maple panels on the drawers of this mahogany, poplar, and yellow pine Neoclassical work stand are a decorative feature more commonly associated with New England furniture. Its leg turnings, however, resemble those of another two-drawer stand found in Charleston. Because yellow pine was not used extensively in Charleston in the early nineteenth century, this piece probably was made elsewhere in South Carolina, particularly since it has an upcountry South Carolina history. *Acc. 3077.*

FA

76 Chest, eastern Tennessee, 1820–30. Furniture made in the Appalachian region of northwestern Tennessee, from Sullivan to Greene counties, reveals a considerable development of regional style with strong roots in both the Shenandoah Valley of Virginia and piedmont North Carolina. The small walnut chest illustrated here, however, is difficult to attribute to any given county or town. Its inlay is related to other Tennessee furniture, but its joined construction suggests a rural mountain origin. The use of nailed leather straps—here replaced—for hinges reinforces this supposition; the brick house replete with chimney inlaid on the front may simply represent the maker's fancy or aspirations. This intriguing dwelling, on a panel made to slide out, is executed in a style not unlike that used on needlework samplers of the period. The intended use of the piece is unknown. *Acc. 2500.*

JB

77 Jug, alkaline-glazed, attributed to Daniel Seagle, Catawba County, North Carolina, 1830–40. This alkaline- or ash-glazed jug has the number 5 impressed over one handle and "D S" over the other. Attributed to Daniel Seagle, who worked in Catawba County from 1827 to 1850, it was probably made in the early part of that period. Its shape resembles that of several pieces made in Edgefield County, South Carolina; one Edgefield storage jar in particular, made by Milton Rhodes at the Collin Rhodes Pottery about 1850, is very like this example.

Although the use of alkaline glaze extended throughout the South and as far west as Texas, it was not used anywhere north of North Carolina, and the Catawba Valley seems to be the only area of North Carolina where alkaline-glazed pottery was produced. *Acc. 2916-3.*   FA

78 Jug, stoneware with alkaline glaze, by Drake Rhodes & Co., Edgefield County, South Carolina, 1836. About 1810 Abner Landrum established a pottery north of Edgefield Courthouse and began making stoneware. He was still operating the business in 1826 when Robert Mills wrote: "There is another village . . . within a mile and a half of Edgefield Court House, called the Pottery or Pottersville . . . altogether supported by the manufacture of Stoneware, carried on by this gentleman [Landrum]." Harvey and Reuben Drake acquired Landrum's pottery in 1827 and operated it until Harvey died in 1832. Collin Rhodes then joined the business, and in January 1836 Nathaniel Ramey became the third partner of "Drake Rhodes & Co.," which operated until September of that year.

This jug is inscribed "Drake Rhodes & Co./ Improved Stoneware/ Edgefield Ct. H. S. C./ 1836" in cobalt slip, a decoration not typical of Edgefield County work. Its ash-gray color may have been the result of a misfiring. The Edgefield potters generally used kaolin or iron decoration on their alkaline-glazed stoneware (80).

Mr. and Mrs. John L. Booth Purchase Fund, acc. 3308.   FA

79 Jug, alkaline-glazed stoneware with slip decoration, impressed "PHOENIX Factory ED. SC," Edgefield County, 1840–42. Collin Rhodes and Robert W. Mathis established the Phoenix Factory in April 1840, and in the fall of that year Rhodes sold his interest in the factory to his brother Coleman. Coleman Rhodes and Mathis then apparently ran the pottery until 1842. The reverse of this jug is impressed with an "L," probably for Amos Landrum, Rhodes's father-in-law, Abner Landrum's brother (79), and very likely one of the pottery's workmen. The Phoenix Factory has been credited with originating the Edgefield decorating tradition exemplified by the brushed iron and kaolin slip of this jug. *Acc. 1054-3.*   FA